REVENUE MANAGEMENT FOR RURAL HOTELS

DAVID SANDUA

"Success in hospitality is based on the ability to deliver a unique and memorable guest experience."

Horst Schulze

INDEX

I. INTRODUCTION

Revenue management is a critical aspect of running a successful hotel business, regardless of its location. For rural hotels, it can be particularly challenging due to various factors unique to their setting. In this essay, we will explore the importance of revenue management for rural hotels and discuss the strategies and techniques that can be implemented to optimize revenue generation. By understanding and implementing effective revenue management practices, rural hotels can overcome the challenges they face and maximize their profitability. It is crucial for rural hotel owners and managers to develop a solid understanding of revenue management principles and apply them in their day-to-day operations. In the following sections, we will delve into the specific challenges faced by rural hotels and examine the various revenue management strategies that can be employed to address these challenges. We will also explore the role of technology in revenue management and its potential to enhance the overall performance of rural hotels. We will provide recommendations and best practices for rural hotel owners and managers to optimize revenue generation. This essay aims to shed light on the significance of revenue management in the context of rural hotels and provide practical insights for improving their financial performance.

DEFINITION OF REVENUE MANAGEMENT

Revenue management refers to the strategic practice of maximizing revenue and optimizing profit for a business. It involves the systematic process of pricing products and services to achieve a balance between customer satisfaction and business profitability. This practice is particularly important in the hospitality industry, where hotels face the challenge of maximizing revenue while meeting the varying demands of their guests. Revenue management requires analyzing data and market trends to set prices at different times and for different segments of customers. By understanding consumer preferences and behavior, hotels can effectively allocate their resources and influence demand. This allows them to offer different rates and packages based on factors such as seasonality, day of the week, and anticipated demand. In essence, revenue management involves finding the optimal price for each product or service in order to achieve maximum profitability. By implementing revenue management strategies effectively, hotels can ultimately increase their market share, attract a broader customer base, and enhance financial performance. Revenue management is an essential tool for hotels to remain competitive in today's dynamic and ever-changing marketplace. It enables them to adapt to fluctuations in demand and make informed decisions about pricing, inventory control, and marketing strategies. By carefully analyzing market conditions and customer behavior, hotels can optimize their revenue potential and maximize profitability. Thus, revenue management is an indispensable practice for hotels seeking long-term success in the industry.

11

IMPORTANCE OF REVENUE MANAGEMENT FOR HOTELS

An essential aspect of running a successful hotel business, especially in a rural area, is revenue management. Revenue management involves optimizing the pricing and availability of hotel rooms to maximize revenue and profitability. By implementing revenue management strategies, hotels can effectively respond to changes in demand, market conditions, and customer preferences. For rural hotels, revenue management is particularly crucial due to the seasonal nature of tourism in these areas. During peak seasons, such as holidays or local festivals, hotels in rural areas experience high demand and can command higher room rates. Conversely, during low seasons, hotels may struggle to attract guests and may need to lower prices to remain competitive. By using revenue management techniques, rural hotels can determine the optimal pricing structure and build strategies to increase occupancy rates during slow periods. Revenue management allows hotels to identify and target specific customer segments, such as business travelers or vacationing families, by offering tailored packages and promotions. By effectively managing revenue, rural hotels can stabilize their operations and ensure long-term sustainability even in the face of fluctuating demand and market conditions. Revenue management plays a vital role in the success of rural hotels by enabling them to adapt to changing market dynamics, optimize pricing strategies, and attract target customer segments. Its importance cannot be overstated in the highly competitive hospitality industry, where maximizing profits while maintaining guest satisfaction is paramount. In order to thrive in now's dynamic and unpredictable market rural hotels must embrace revenue management as integral part of their overall business strategy.

REVENUE MANAGEMENT STRATEGIES FOR RURAL HOTELS

In order for rural hotels to maximize their revenue potential, it is crucial to have a thorough understanding of revenue management strategies. One such strategy is the implementation of dynamic pricing. This involves adjusting room rates based on factors such as demand, seasonality, and local events. During peak travel seasons or popular events in the rural area, hotels can optimize their revenue by increasing their room rates. Conversely, during slower periods or off-seasons, hotels can attract more guests by offering discounted rates. Another key revenue management strategy for rural hotels is the effective use of distribution channels. By leveraging various online travel agencies and booking platforms, rural hotels can expand their reach and attract a wider customer base. Hotels can also explore partnerships with local tourism organizations and travel agents to increase their visibility to potential guests. Implementing effective marketing strategies is essential for revenue maximization. Rural hotels can utilize targeted marketing campaigns to reach specific customer segments, such as couples looking for romantic getaways or families seeking outdoor adventures. By tailoring their marketing messages and promotions to these segments, hotels can attract more bookings and increase their revenue. Rural hotels can differentiate themselves and attract more guests by offering unique experiences and amenities. This can include organizing guided tours of the local area, providing farm-to-table dining experiences with locally sourced ingredients, or offering outdoor activities such as hiking or fishing. By

15

creating memorable experiences for guests rural hotels can increase their chances of repeat visits and positive word-of-mouth recommendations which can drive higher revenues. Furthermore it is crucial for rural hotels to effectively manage their inventory to maximize their revenue. This can be achieved by the use of yield management techniques such as adjusting minimum night stays implementing restrictions on certain room types or introducing package deals to encourage longer stays. By managing their inventory strategically hotels can maximize their revenue potential and ensure optimal occupancy levels. The last thing it is important for rural hotels to invest in technology and data analytics to support their revenue management efforts. Using revenue management software and systems hotels can provide valuable insights into market trends customer preference and booking patterns. This data can be used to make a cost effective forecast take and identify areas for improvement. In general rural hotels need to take a comprehensive revenue management approach that includes dynamic pricing effective distribution targeted marketing personalized experiences inventory management and technology to maximize their revenue potential and ensure long-term success.

II. UNDERSTANDING THE MARKET

One crucial aspect of revenue management for a rural hotel is understanding the market. In order for a hotel to effectively manage its revenue, it must have a thorough understanding of the market in which it operates. This includes understanding the demand patterns, the competition, and the overall market trends. By understanding the demand patterns, the hotel can adjust its pricing and availability to maximize revenue. If the hotel knows that weekends are high-demand periods, it can increase prices for those nights to capture additional revenue. Conversely, if mid-weekdays tend to have lower demand, the hotel can offer promotions or discounted rates to attract more guests during those times. Understanding the competition is essential for revenue management. By analyzing the pricing strategies and offerings of competitors, the hotel can position itself competitively and make pricing decisions accordingly. If a nearby hotel is offering a lower rate for a similar room type, the hotel can consider adjusting its rates to remain competitive. Keeping track of market trends is vital for revenue management. This includes staying informed about major events or festivals in the area that might impact demand for hotel rooms. By knowing about these trends in advance, the hotel can make proactive adjustments to its pricing and availability to capture the increased demand. Understanding the market is a fundamental component of revenue management, as it allows the hotel to make informed decisions about pricing, promotion, and inventory control.

CONDUCTING MARKET RESEARCH TO IDENTIFY TARGET CUSTOMERS

While conducting market research is crucial for any business, it holds particular significance for a rural hotel. In order to effectively identify target customers, a comprehensive approach should be adopted. One important aspect of market research involves analyzing demographics. By examining factors such as age, income level, and location, the hotel can gain insights into the profile of their potential customers. If the research reveals that the majority of visitors to the area are older adults seeking a peaceful retreat, the hotel can tailor its services and amenities to cater to this specific demographic. Conducting market research allows the hotel to identify trends and preferences among potential customers. This can be achieved through surveys, interviews, or through studying market reports and industry publications. By unearthing information about customer preferences, such as preferred activities, dietary requirements, or specific amenities desired, the hotel can further customize its offerings to appeal to its target market. Analyzing competitor activities within the rural hotel market is another critical component of market research. By studying competitors' strategies, offerings, and pricing, the hotel can gain a competitive edge and ensure that their own offerings are unique and appealing to the target customers. Market research can help the hotel identify any gaps or untapped opportunities in the market, which can lead to innovative strategies and new revenue sources. If research reveals a lack of family-friendly accommodation options in the area For example the hotel could consider adding family

19

suites or offering special packages and activities For children. Using market research in general helps rural hotels build a deep understanding of their target customers allowing them to customize their offerings and strategies to better meet their needs and preferences. The hotel can place itself as the top choice for its target customers By analyzing demographics identifying trends and preferences studying competitors and identifying gaps in the market this will lead to increased revenue and success in the market.

ANALYZING COMPETITORS AND THEIR PRICING STRATEGIES

By understanding how competitors price their rooms and services, a hotel can position itself strategically in the market and optimize its revenue. One way to analyze competitors is by conducting a competitive analysis, which involves evaluating various aspects such as pricing, offerings, and target market. By examining the competitors' pricing strategies, a hotel can identify potential opportunities for differentiation and competitive advantage. If most competitors in the area offer high-end luxury accommodations at premium prices, a rural hotel can focus on attracting price-sensitive customers by offering affordable yet comfortable rooms. On the other hand, if competitors have positioned themselves as budget-friendly options, the rural hotel can differentiate itself by offering unique experiences or additional amenities to attract customers willing to pay a premium. Analyzing competitors' pricing strategies can help a hotel determine the optimal price points for its own offerings. If competitors have consistently high prices during peak seasons and low prices during off-peak periods, the rural hotel can consider implementing dynamic pricing strategies to adjust its rates accordingly. By offering competitive prices during high-demand periods and lower prices during low-demand periods, the hotel can attract a wide range of customers while maximizing revenue. Analyzing competitors' pricing strategies can provide insights into market trends and fluctuations. In monitoring the price changes of competitors a hotel can identify trends and adjust its own pricing strategy accordingly. If competition is

21

consistently raising their prices this may indicate an increase in demand and the hotel can consider adjusting its rates to capture additional revenue. Conversely if competitors are lowering their prices this may indicate a decrease in demand and the hotel can adjust its rates to remain competitive and attract customers. In addition the analysis of competition s pricing strategies can help a rural hotel value its own value proposition. The hotel can place areas where it can improve itself By comparing what the competitors offer with the hotel's offer. For example if competitors offer a free breakfast the rural hotel can consider implementing a similar provide to increase its value proposition and attract more customers. Analyzing competitors and their pricing strategies are therefore an essential part of revenue management for a rural hotel. By understanding market dynamics finding potential opportunities and remaining competitive a hotel can optimize its revenue and maintain a sustainable business in a rural setting.

IDENTIFYING UNIQUE SELLING POINTS OF THE RURAL HOTEL

In order to effectively implement revenue management strategies for a rural hotel, it is crucial to identify the unique selling points that set it apart from other accommodations in the area. These unique selling points can serve as key differentiators and attract specific target markets. One potential unique selling point of a rural hotel may be its picturesque surroundings and tranquil ambiance. This can appeal to guests who are seeking an escape from the hustle and bustle of city life. Offering guests the opportunity to reconnect with nature and enjoy outdoor activities such as hiking, biking, or fishing can further enhance the appeal of the rural hotel. The hotel's location may be in close proximity to popular tourist attractions or landmarks, which can be highlighted as another unique selling point. Guests who are interested in exploring the local culture and history may be drawn to a rural hotel that provides easy access to these attractions. A rural hotel may differentiate itself through its personalized service and attention to detail. Small details such as welcoming guests by name, anticipating their needs, and offering personalized recommendations for local activities or dining options can create a memorable experience for guests and increase their likelihood of returning or recommending the hotel to others. Another unique selling point can be the hotel's focus on sustainability and eco-friendly practices. Many travelers are becoming increasingly aware of their environmental impact and actively seek accommodation that aligns with their values. Through the implementation of green initiatives such as energy-efficient lighting recycling programs and locally-sourced produce a rural hotel can attract environmentally-minded guests and position itself as a responsible and sustainable choice. A rural hotel may further possess a unique selling point in the form of its facilities and amenities on site. This can include a fitness center spa swimming pool or a restaurant that offers farm-to-table meals. By highlighting these amenities a rural hotel can appeal to guests who desire a kind of recreational activities or a convenient dining get without giving the place. Finally a rural hotel may distinguish itself through partnerships or cooperations with local businesses artisans or farmers. This can include showing and selling local products or offering unique experiences such as farm tours or cooking classes. By promoting these partnerships a rural hotel can attract guests who are interested in supporting local economies and experiencing local culture. For successful revenue management it is essential to identify the unique selling points of a rural hotel. By understanding what differentiates the hotel from competitors specific marketing strategies can be developed to attract specific guest segments. Each unique selling point adds value to the rural hotel have and can bring to its long-term success Whether it is the picturesque surroundings personalized service eco-friendly practices on site amenities or local partnerships.

III. PRICING STRATEGIES

One effective pricing strategy is differential pricing, which involves charging different prices for the same product or service based on factors such as demand, time of year, or customer segment. During peak seasons when demand is high, the hotel can charge a premium price for its rooms. On the other hand, during off-peak seasons when demand is low, the hotel can offer discounted rates to attract customers. This strategy helps optimize revenue by maximizing revenue during periods of high demand and minimizing revenue loss during periods of low demand. Another pricing strategy to consider is dynamic pricing, which involves adjusting prices based on real-time data and market conditions. With the help of technology, hotels can monitor demand patterns, competitor prices, and other market factors to determine the optimal price for their rooms. By setting prices that align with the demand and value perception of customers, the hotel can maximize revenue and profitability. In addition to differential pricing and dynamic pricing, another strategy to consider is price bundling. Price bundling involves selling multiple products or services together as a package at a discounted price. A rural hotel can offer a weekend getaway package that includes accommodation, meals, and recreational activities at a lower price than if these items were purchased individually. Price bundling not only incentivizes customers to purchase more, but it also helps the hotel increase occupancy and revenue by selling a combination of services. Implementing a demand-based pricing strategy can be beneficial for a rural hotel. Demand-based pricing involves setting prices based on the specific dates and times when demand is highest or lowest. A hotel located near a popular tourist attraction may charge higher rates during peak travel seasons and lower rates during shoulder seasons to attract more guests. By adjusting prices based on demand patterns, the hotel can capitalize on periods of high demand and offer competitive prices during periods of low demand to attract budget-conscious travelers. Implementing a tiered pricing strategy can be effective for a rural hotel. Tiered pricing involves offering different levels of service or amenities at various price points. A hotel can offer standard rooms at a lower price, while also providing upgraded rooms or suites at higher price points. This strategy allows the hotel to cater to different customer segments with varying budgets and preferences. By offering a range of options, the hotel can capture a broader market and generate more revenue. Pricing strategies are essential for revenue management in a rural hotel. Differential pricing, dynamic pricing, price bundling, demand-based pricing, and tiered pricing are all effective strategies that can help optimize revenue and maximize profitability. By carefully assessing market conditions, customer preferences, and the hotel's unique selling points, rural hotels can implement pricing strategies that attract customers, increase occupancy rates, and ultimately drive revenue growth.

SETTING COMPETITIVE PRICES BASED ON MARKET ANALYSIS

Market analysis involves studying the pricing strategies of competitors, consumer demand, and economic factors that can influence pricing. By conducting a thorough analysis, a hotel can determine the ideal price range that not only attracts customers but also provides a reasonable profit margin. The first step in setting competitive prices is to evaluate the offerings and prices of similar hotels in the area. This can be done by researching online, analyzing brochures or marketing materials, or even making personal visits to the competition. By understanding the prices charged by competitors, a hotel can determine where it stands in comparison and make adjustments accordingly. Analyzing consumer demand is crucial to setting competitive prices. Market research can help identify peak and off-peak seasons, as well as specific events or attractions that attract tourists to the area. This knowledge allows the hotel to adjust prices depending on the level of demand, maximizing revenue during high-demand periods and attracting customers during low-demand periods. Economic factors also play a significant role in setting competitive prices. Factors such as inflation, currency exchange rates, and economic stability can influence the purchasing power of consumers and their willingness to pay certain prices. It is important for a hotel to consider these factors when setting prices to ensure they are both attractive to customers and sustainable for the business. Setting competitive prices for a rural hotel based on market analysis requires a thorough un-

27

derstanding of the competition, consumer demand, and economic factors. By conducting a comprehensive analysis, a hotel can determine the ideal price range that attracts customers and provides a reasonable profit margin. This approach allows the hotel to maximize revenue and stay competitive in the industry.

UTILIZING DYNAMIC PRICING TO MAXIMIZE REVENUE

Dynamic pricing is a valuable strategy for maximizing revenue in the hospitality industry. By adjusting prices in real-time based on factors such as demand, availability, and market conditions, hotels can effectively optimize their revenue potential. Implemented correctly, dynamic pricing can result in higher room rates during peak periods and lower rates during periods of lower demand, ensuring that hotels can maximize revenue across all seasons. Dynamic pricing allows hotels to take advantage of changing market conditions by quickly adjusting prices to reflect current supply and demand. This ability to adapt pricing in real-time ensures that hotels are not losing out on potential revenue during periods of high demand or leaving rooms empty during periods of low demand. Dynamic pricing can be employed to target specific customer segments and optimize revenue from different market segments. By strategically adjusting prices based on demand patterns from various customer segments, hotels can attract a wider range of customers without compromising overall revenue. It gives hotels the flexibility to offer discounts to price-sensitive customers while charging higher rates to customers willing to pay a premium. This targeted pricing approach allows hotels to maximize revenue by catering to the needs of different market segments and effectively monetizing their product offerings. Dynamic pricing can help hotels to manage uncertainty and minimize the risk of revenue loss due to last-minute cancellations or no-shows. By setting different booking policies and adjusting prices based on these policies, hotels can incentivize guests to book non-refundable rates or prepaid reservations, reducing the chances of cancellations and minimizing revenue losses. Dynamic pricing can help hotels to optimize revenue from ancillary services and upselling opportunities. By adjusting the prices of add-ons, such as breakfast packages, Wi-Fi access, or room upgrades, hotels can capture additional revenue from guests who are willing to pay for these services. This not only increases the overall revenue but also enhances the guest experience by providing them with the option to customize their stay according to their preferences and budget. Dynamic pricing can be applied to other revenue streams in the hotel, such as the sale of event spaces, meeting rooms, or spa services. By adjusting prices based on demand and availability, hotels can optimize revenue from these non-room revenue sources as well. Utilizing dynamic pricing is a crucial revenue management strategy for hotels, particularly in the rural context. By adjusting prices in real-time, hotels can maximize revenue potential, adapt to changing market conditions, target specific customer segments, mitigate risks, optimize revenue from ancillary services, and capitalize on non-room revenue sources. With the right tools and strategies in place, hotels can effectively implement dynamic pricing and unlock their full revenue potential.

IMPLEMENTING PRICE DIFFERENTIATION BASED ON CUSTOMER SEGMENTS

Implementing price differentiation based on customer segments is another key strategy for revenue management in a rural hotel. By analyzing the different customer segments and their willingness to pay, the hotel can adjust its pricing to maximize revenue. Business travelers may be willing to pay a higher price for the convenience and amenities provided, while leisure travelers might be more price-sensitive. The hotel can offer special packages or discounts for families or groups, attracting a higher number of bookings and increasing occupancy rates during quieter periods. The hotel can target specific segments during off-peak seasons, such as offering discounted rates for senior citizens or special packages for couples on romantic getaways. By tailoring the pricing strategy to different customer segments, the hotel can optimize its revenue and achieve a balance between attracting new customers and maximizing profitability. Employing dynamic pricing techniques can also be beneficial in this regard. By continuously monitoring and adjusting prices based on factors such as demand, supply, and competitor prices, the hotel can respond to market fluctuations and capitalize on opportunities to increase revenue. During periods of high demand, the hotel can raise prices to capture the full value from customers willing to pay more. On the other hand, during low demand periods, the hotel can offer discounted rates to stimulate demand and attract customers who might otherwise choose alternative accommodations. Using advanced analytics and technology, the hotel can implement real-time pricing strategies that allow for instantaneous adjustments in response to market changes. If the hotel notices a sudden increase in demand for a particular room type, it can quickly raise the price to capitalize on the increased willingness to pay. Conversely, if there is a sudden decrease in demand, the hotel can immediately lower the price to mitigate any potential revenue loss. Implementing price differentiation based on customer segments and utilizing dynamic pricing techniques not only helps the hotel maximize revenue but also improves the overall guest experience. By offering tailored pricing options, customers feel they are getting the best value for their money, which increases customer satisfaction and loyalty. Through increased revenue, the hotel can invest in further improving its facilities and services, enhancing the guest experience even more. By consistently analyzing customer preferences and adjusting pricing accordingly, the hotel can maintain a competitive edge in a rural market and increase its market share. Implementing price differentiation based on customer segments and utilizing dynamic pricing strategies are crucial for revenue management in a rural hotel. By understanding the needs and preferences of different customer segments, the hotel can tailor its pricing to maximize revenue while offering the best value to its guests. The use of advanced analytics and real-time pricing techniques enables the hotel to adapt quickly to market changes and leverage demand fluctuations to optimize revenue. Through these strategies, not only can the hotel increase profitability but also enhance the overall guest experience, foster customer loyalty, and gain a competitive advantage in the rural market.

IV. DEMAND FORECASTING

Demand forecasting is an essential aspect of revenue management for a rural hotel as it allows the establishment to anticipate and plan future demand patterns. The hotel can accurately predict demand for its rooms and adjust their pricing strategies By analyzing historical data and market trends. This forecasting process involves the use of various analytical tools and techniques to estimate future demand for specific periods such as daily weekly or monthly. Demand forecasting also takes into account several factors that can influence demand including seasonality local events and economic conditions. By understanding these factors and accurately forecasting demand rural hotels can maximize their revenue By balancing the supply of rooms with expected demand. This enables the business to maximize occupancy rates and revenue potential. A modern demand forecasting system also allows hotel managers to take informed decisions regarding inventory and pricing strategies. For example if the forecast indicates a high demand For a specific period the hotel can implement dynamic pricing strategies such as increasing the rates For rooms or imposing minimum stays. On the other hand if forecast a lower demand the hotel can introduce promotional offers or discounts to attract more customers. Demand forecasting additionally assists in the management of operational costs. By accurately anticipating demand the hotel can optimize its workforce and other resources to meet the expected demand efficiently. This ensures that the hotel is adequately staffed during peak periods while reducing costs during periods of lower demand. Demand forecasting plays a crucial role in revenue management for a rural hotel and contributes to its overall success. It enables the establishment to allocate resources effectively, optimize pricing strategies, and respond proactively to changing market conditions. Demand forecasting also facilitates effective marketing and promotional activities. By understanding the expected demand, the hotel can design targeted marketing campaigns to attract customers during periods of low demand or promote special packages during high-demand periods. This strategic approach not only helps the hotel maintain a steady revenue stream but also build customer loyalty and enhance its brand reputation. Demand forecasting is an integral part of revenue management for a rural hotel. It allows hotels to predict future demand patterns, optimize pricing strategies, manage operational costs, and engage in effective marketing activities. By accurately forecasting demand, hotels can effectively plan and allocate resources, maximize occupancy rates, and achieve sustainable revenue growth. Consequently, demand forecasting is essential for the long-term success and profitability of rural hotels.

COLLECTING AND ANALYZING HISTORICAL DATA ON ROOM BOOKINGS

Another important aspect of revenue management for a rural hotel is the collection and analysis of historical data on room bookings. By collecting data on previous bookings, a hotel can develop a better understanding of demand patterns and make informed decisions on pricing and inventory management. By analyzing historical data, the hotel can identify peak seasons and low-demand periods, allowing them to adjust room rates accordingly. The data collected can also help in identifying trends and patterns, such as the popularity of certain room types or the impact of local events on bookings. By having access to this information, the hotel can optimize its revenue by offering targeted promotions, adjusting inventory levels, and improving overall efficiency. Historical data can be used to forecast future demand and set achievable revenue targets. By analyzing trends and patterns, the hotel can make informed predictions about future bookings and adjust its strategies accordingly. If the data suggests that a particular event will attract a large number of guests, the hotel can proactively increase room rates and allocate more inventory to maximize revenue. On the other hand, if the data shows a decline in bookings during a certain period, the hotel can offer discounted rates or special packages to attract more guests. The collection and analysis of historical data on room bookings is crucial for a rural hotel to implement effective revenue management strategies and maximize its profitability.

USING FORECASTING TECHNIQUES TO PREDICT FUTURE DEMAND

Forecasting techniques are essential in predicting future demand in revenue management for a rural hotel. These techniques involve analyzing historical data and trends to make accurate predictions about future consumer behavior. One such technique is the time series analysis, which involves examining patterns and fluctuations in demand over a specific time period. This information can then be used to make informed decisions about pricing and inventory management. Regression analysis can be employed to identify the relationship between demand and other variables, such as seasonality, social events, and economic factors. By understanding these relationships, hotels can adjust their pricing and promotional strategies accordingly. Another effective technique is the use of market research and customer surveys to gather insights about customer preferences, habits, and booking patterns. By directly engaging with customers and understanding their needs, hotels can anticipate future demand and tailor their offerings to meet expectations. Predictive modeling techniques, such as artificial intelligence and machine learning algorithms, can be utilized to analyze vast amounts of data and generate accurate forecasts. These advanced techniques can account for complex variables and market dynamics to provide hotels with valuable insights into future demand. By employing various forecasting techniques, revenue managers can make informed decisions to optimize revenues and maximize profitability.

ADJUSTING PRICING AND AVAILABILITY BASED ON DEMAND FORECASTS

In addition to optimizing revenue through customer segmentation and effective distribution strategies, another key component of revenue management for a rural hotel is adjusting pricing and availability based on demand forecasts. By accurately predicting future demand, hotels can strategically adjust their pricing and availability to maximize revenue. One method of demand forecasting is by analyzing historical data and trends to identify patterns and make informed predictions about future demand. This can include analyzing data such as booking patterns, seasonality, and local events that may impact demand. By gaining insights from this data, hotels can make more accurate forecasts and adjust their pricing accordingly. If historical data shows that there is typically high demand during a particular time of year due to a local festival, the hotel can increase their prices during that period to capitalize on the increased demand. On the other hand, if historical data shows that there is typically low demand during a particular season, the hotel can adjust their pricing to attract more guests during that time. Hotels can use dynamic pricing strategies to adjust prices in real-time based on demand fluctuations. This can involve using revenue management systems that take into account factors such as occupancy levels, competitor pricing, and market conditions to determine optimal pricing. By constantly monitoring and adjusting prices based on demand, hotels can ensure they are maximizing revenue and optimizing occupancy levels. Adjusting availability based on demand forecasts is another important aspect of revenue management. By closely monitoring demand forecasts, hotels can strategically open or close room inventory to effectively manage supply and demand. If demand is projected to be high during a certain period, the hotel can release more rooms for sale to meet the anticipated demand. Conversely, if demand is projected to be low, the hotel can limit room availability to create a sense of scarcity and potentially increase prices. This approach helps ensure that the hotel is maximizing revenue by aligning supply with demand. Employing different rate categories can also help in adjusting availability. By offering different rate categories such as advanced purchase rates or non-refundable rates, hotels can incentivize guests to book early or commit to their stay, ensuring a more accurate demand forecast and helping the hotel manage inventory more effectively. Adjusting pricing and availability based on demand forecasts is a crucial aspect of revenue management for a rural hotel. By accurately predicting future demand and utilizing methods such as historical data analysis and dynamic pricing strategies, hotels can optimize their pricing to maximize revenue. By strategically adjusting room availability based on demand forecasts and employing different rate categories, hotels can effectively manage their supply and demand, ensuring they are maximizing revenue and optimizing occupancy levels. Effective revenue management practices can ultimately make a rural hotel the success and profitability.

V. INVENTORY MANAGEMENT

Effective inventory management ensures that a hotel has the right amount of rooms available at the right time to maximize revenue. A hotel's inventory includes not only its guest rooms but also its meeting and event spaces, parking spaces, and other facilities. The hotel must carefully analyze its demand patterns and take into account seasonal variations, holidays, and local events to determine the optimal allocation of inventory. By understanding and anticipating demand fluctuations, the hotel can make informed decisions about pricing, availability, and restrictions. During peak periods, such as holidays or popular local events, the hotel may implement restrictions on minimum lengths of stay or require non-refundable reservations to ensure optimal occupancy and maximize revenue. Conversely, during periods of low demand, the hotel may offer discounted rates or flexible cancellation policies to attract more guests. Effective inventory management also involves monitoring and adjusting inventory levels in real-time. This can be achieved through the use of a Property Management System (PMS) that integrates with the hotel's Central Reservation System. The PMS provides an accurate and up-to-date view of the hotel's inventory, allowing the revenue manager to make dynamic pricing decisions and optimize revenue. The PMS can generate reports and analytics that enable the hotel to identify trends, forecast demand, and adjust inventory levels accordingly. By effectively managing its inventory, a rural hotel can ensure that it is attracting the right guests at the right price, maximizing revenue, and maintaining a competitive edge in the market.

OPTIMIZING ROOM AVAILABILITY TO MAXIMIZE REVENUE

One way to optimize room availability and maximize revenue for a rural hotel is by implementing a dynamic pricing strategy. This strategy involves adjusting room rates based on demand and market conditions. By dynamically pricing rooms, hotels can ensure that they are charging the optimal rate at any given time to maximize revenue. During a peak season or weekends, when demand is high, hotels can increase their rates to capture the maximum value from each room. On the other hand, during slower periods or weekdays, hotels can offer discounted rates to attract more guests and fill empty rooms. Another strategy to optimize room availability is by offering different packages or promotions. By creating attractive packages or promotions, hotels can entice guests to book a room even during periods of low demand. A hotel could offer a weekend getaway package that includes accommodations, breakfast, and a spa treatment at a discounted rate. This type of promotion not only attracts more guests but also encourages them to spend more money on additional services and amenities. Hotels can consider implementing a minimum length of stay requirement during high-demand periods. By setting a minimum length of stay, hotels can ensure that they are maximizing revenue by filling rooms for longer periods. For example during holidays or special events hotels may require a minimum of two nights of accommodation to accommodate guests who are willing to pay a premium rate For their desired dates. In addition technology investments and online distribution channels can greatly optimize room availability. By using a robust property management system and interacting with online travel agencies hotels can automate inventory management and maximize potential guests exposure. This allows hotels to take control of room availability and pricing in real-time ensuring that they don't miss out on any revenue opportunities. For attracting more potential customers Hotels can leverage social media and digital marketing. By using these tools hotels can continuously optimize room availability and increase revenue. Optimization of room availability is crucial for maximizing revenue for a rural hotel In conclusion. The hotel can ensure that its rooms are always in high demand By implementing dynamic pricing strategies offering attractive packages and promotions setting minimum length of stay requirements and investing in technology. They not only help maximize revenues but also enhance guest satisfaction by providing them with value added services and experiences. In the end rural hotels can prosper in a competitive market and achieve long-term success by carefully managing room availability.

IMPLEMENTING OVERBOOKING STRATEGIES TO MINIMIZE REVENUE LOSS

Overbooking refers to the practice of accepting more reservations than the hotel can accommodate, assuming that some guests will cancel or fail to show up. By implementing overbooking strategies, hotels can maximize their occupancy rates and reduce the financial impact of cancellations or no-shows. One such strategy is forecasting demand accurately by analyzing historical data, market trends, and events happening in the local area. By understanding demand patterns, hotels can estimate the probability of cancellations or no-shows and adjust their overbooking levels accordingly. Hotels can use sophisticated revenue management systems that automate the process of tracking cancellations and no-shows, allowing them to respond quickly and reallocate rooms to new guests. These systems can also integrate data from online travel agencies and other distribution channels, providing a comprehensive view of bookings and cancellations. Another overbooking strategy is offering guests incentives to voluntarily give up their reservation if the hotel faces an overcapacity situation. These incentives can include upgrades, discounts on future stays, or complimentary services. By incentivizing guests to give up their reservation, hotels can avoid any negative impact on customer satisfaction while still maximizing occupancy and revenue. It is essential to communicate transparently and maintain good customer relationships during this process. Hotels can also leverage technology to optimize their overbooking strategies. Dynamic pricing algorithms can adjust room rates in real-time based on demand

and availability. By continuously updating prices, hotels can attract new bookings and respond to cancellations or no-shows promptly. Hotels can use predictive analytics tools to determine the optimal overbooking level based on various factors such as historical data, market conditions, and customer behavior. These tools can help generate insights and make data-driven decisions to maximize revenue while minimizing the risk of overbooking. Implementing overbooking strategies is a valuable technique for hotels to minimize revenue loss. By accurately forecasting demand, using advanced revenue management systems, offering incentives, and leveraging technology, hotels can optimize their occupancy rates and reduce the impact of cancellations or no-shows. It is crucial for hotels to strike a balance between maximizing revenue and maintaining good customer relationships. Overbooking strategies are a vital component of revenue management for hotels, particularly in a rural setting where demand might be more unpredictable.

MANAGING ROOM ALLOCATIONS FOR DIFFERENT CUSTOMER SEGMENTS

By strategically allocating rooms based on customer segments, a hotel can maximize its revenue potential. One way to manage room allocations is by analyzing historical data and identifying patterns within each customer segment. This analysis can help the hotel understand which segments tend to book larger or more expensive rooms, and which segments are more likely to book last-minute or discounted rates. Armed with this information, the hotel can adjust its room availability to meet the demands of each segment. If the hotel knows that business travelers often book larger rooms, it can prioritize these room types for this segment. On the other hand, if families tend to book last-minute and take advantage of discounted rates, the hotel can save a certain number of rooms for this segment closer to the arrival date. By tailoring room allocations to the specific needs and behaviors of each customer segment, the hotel can increase its overall revenue. Another strategy for managing room allocations is by implementing a tiered pricing system. This involves categorizing rooms into different tiers and assigning different prices to each tier. The hotel can classify its rooms into standard, deluxe, and premium tiers, with corresponding price points. This allows the hotel to cater to different customer segments with varying budgets. By offering a range of room options, the hotel can appeal to both cost-conscious customers seeking more affordable accommodations and customers willing to pay a premium for higher-end rooms. A tiered pricing system can create a sense of exclusivity and luxury for those willing to splurge on upgraded accommodations. This not only increases revenue but also enhances the overall guest experience, as customers have more choices that align with their preferences and budget. To effectively manage room allocations for different customer segments, a hotel must adopt technology solutions that facilitate dynamic pricing and inventory management. Revenue management systems provide real-time data and analytics, allowing the hotel to make informed decisions about room allocations based on demand and market conditions. These systems can also automate the process of adjusting prices and availability, enabling the hotel to respond quickly to changes in demand and optimize revenue potential. By investing in the right technology, a rural hotel can streamline its room allocation process and ensure that rooms are allocated based on data-driven insights. Managing room allocations for different customer segments is crucial for revenue management in a rural hotel. By analyzing historical data, implementing a tiered pricing system, and leveraging technology solutions, a hotel can optimize its room allocation strategy to maximize revenue. By catering to the specific needs and preferences of each customer segment, the hotel can enhance guest satisfaction and profitability. Embedding a strategic room allocation process within the revenue management framework can help rural hotels thrive in a competitive market.

VI. DISTRIBUTION CHANNELS

These channels serve as intermediaries between the hotel and potential customers, facilitating the booking process and ensuring a wider reach of the hotel's offerings. With the growing prevalence of online booking platforms, hotels need to effectively utilize various distribution channels to maximize their revenue potential. One commonly used distribution channel is online travel agencies (OTAs), such as Expedia, Booking. com, and Airbnb. OTAs provide a platform where customers can easily compare prices and book accommodations. By partnering with these platforms, rural hotels can extend their visibility to a broader audience and attract guests who may not have otherwise discovered their property. Another important distribution channel for hotels is direct bookings through their official websites. By investing in a user-friendly website and implementing online booking capabilities, hotels can encourage customers to book directly, thereby reducing the commission fees associated with third-party channels. Hotels can personalize the booking experience when customers book directly, allowing for upselling and cross-selling opportunities. Hotels can leverage global distribution systems (GDS), which act as a central reservation system connecting hotels to travel agents and online travel agencies worldwide. Through GDS, rural hotels can expand their reach to a wider audience and tap into the extensive network of travel agents. This strategic approach allows hotels to gain exposure to niche markets and attract new customers who prefer to book through traditional travel agencies. Hotels can establish partnerships with tour operators and travel wholesalers to target specific market segments such as group tourists, adventure seekers, or luxury travelers. These partnerships can be mutually beneficial, as hotels can secure a steady stream of bookings, while tour operators and wholesalers can offer bundled packages that include accommodation. Rural hotels can benefit from government tourism boards and local visitor centers that promote regional attractions and accommodations. By collaborating with these organizations, hotels can tap into marketing campaigns, tourism events, and visitor guides that target specific geographical areas or interest groups. In addition to these traditional distribution channels, rural hotels can also embrace newer platforms such as social media influencers and bloggers. These influencers can promote the hotel's unique features and experiences to their followers, generating buzz and attracting potential customers who are seeking authentic and off-the-beaten-track experiences. By diversifying their distribution channels and carefully selecting the most relevant ones, rural hotels can optimize their revenue management strategies and ensure a steady flow of bookings throughout the year.

EVALUATING AND SELECTING APPROPRIATE DISTRIBUTION CHANNELS

When evaluating and selecting appropriate distribution channels for a rural hotel, there are several factors that need to be taken into consideration. Firstly, it is important to consider the target market and their preferred channels for booking accommodations. The hotel should conduct market research to identify the demographics and preferences of potential guests in order to effectively reach them through the most suitable distribution channels. If the target market consists of younger, tech-savvy travelers, it may be beneficial to focus on online travel agencies, social media platforms, and the hotel's own website to maximize exposure and booking opportunities. On the other hand, if the target market is predominantly older individuals who may be less inclined to book online, it may be more effective to establish relationships with local travel agencies or participate in trade shows to gain visibility. Secondly, it is important to evaluate the cost and potential return on investment associated with each distribution channel. Some channels, such as online travel agencies, may charge commission fees for each booking, while others, such as partnering with local travel agencies, may require upfront fees or ongoing commissions. It is crucial to consider the financial implications of each channel and weigh it against the potential revenue it can generate. Thirdly, the hotel should consider the level of control it wants to have over the booking process. Some distribution channels, such as online travel agencies, allow for easy and immediate bookings, but the hotel may have less control over pricing and availability. This

51

can be a disadvantage for a rural hotel that may experience fluctuating demand throughout the year. Conversely, direct bookings through the hotel's own website or phone reservations provide the hotel with greater control over pricing and availability, but may require additional marketing efforts to drive traffic and bookings. It is important to consider the level of customer service and support provided by each distribution channel. When guests book through third-party websites or travel agencies, they may not receive the same level of personalized service and support as they would if they booked directly with the hotel. This can impact the guest experience and overall satisfaction. It is vital to evaluate the reputation and customer service track record of each distribution channel to ensure that it aligns with the hotel's service standards. Evaluating and selecting appropriate distribution channels for a rural hotel requires careful consideration of the target market, cost and return on investment, level of control, and customer service provided. By taking these factors into account, the hotel can make informed decisions that will effectively reach its target market, maximize revenue, and enhance the overall guest experience.

UTILIZING ONLINE TRAVEL AGENCIES AND DIRECT BOOKING PLATFORMS

Another way for rural hotels to increase their revenue is by utilizing online travel agencies (OTAs) and direct booking platforms. OTAs, such as Expedia and Booking. com, have a wide reach and attract a large number of online travelers. By listing their property on these platforms, rural hotels can tap into this extensive customer base and increase their chances of bookings. OTAs often offer promotional opportunities, such as featured listings or discounted rates, which can help attract more potential guests. Direct booking platforms, on the other hand, allow rural hotels to connect directly with their customers without the need for intermediaries. This not only allows for better communication and personalized service but also eliminates the commission fees that OTAs charge. By having their own booking platform, rural hotels can offer exclusive deals and incentives to encourage guests to book directly, thereby maximizing their revenue. It is important for rural hotels to carefully manage their presence on OTAs and direct booking platforms. Having too many listings on various platforms can lead to a loss of control over pricing and availability, which can ultimately affect revenue. It is crucial for hotels to regularly monitor and update their listings to ensure that they reflect accurate information and remain competitive in the market. Hotels should consider their target audience when choosing which platforms to utilize. Some OTAs may cater more towards budget travelers, while others may attract a more high-end clientele. Understanding the preferences and behaviors of their target market can help rural hotels strategically choose the platforms that will generate the greatest return on investment. It is important for hotels to consider the cost implications of utilizing OTAs and direct booking platforms. While OTAs offer a wide customer reach, they also charge commission fees for each booking made through their platform. This fee can significantly impact a hotel's profit margin, especially for smaller rural hotels with limited resources. Direct booking platforms, on the other hand, may require an initial investment to set up and maintain, but they can be a more cost-effective option in the long run. By weighing the potential benefits and costs, rural hotels can make informed decisions on which platforms to utilize to maximize their revenue. Utilizing online travel agencies and direct booking platforms can be a valuable revenue management strategy for rural hotels. These platforms provide access to a large customer base, offer promotional opportunities, and allow for direct communication with guests. Hotels need to carefully manage their presence, consider their target market, and assess the cost implications to ensure the most effective use of these platforms. By doing so, rural hotels can maximize their revenue and stay competitive in the market.

IMPLEMENTING CHANNEL MANAGEMENT STRATEGIES TO OPTIMIZE REVENUE

Implementing channel management strategies is essential for rural hotels to optimize revenue. One effective strategy is to diversify distribution channels by partnering with online travel agencies (OTAs) and global distribution systems (GDS). By utilizing OTAs such as Expedia and Booking. com, rural hotels can tap into their large customer base and increase visibility to potential guests. Similarly, integrating with GDS platforms like Amadeus and Sabre allows rural hotels to reach a wider audience and attract more bookings. Another channel management strategy is to implement rate parity across all distribution channels. This ensures that the hotel's rates are consistent across different platforms, avoiding price discrepancies and maintaining customer trust. Rural hotels can employ the use of revenue management systems (RMS) to automate the distribution of rates and availability across various channels. These systems analyze market conditions, demand patterns, and competitor rates to generate optimal pricing strategies. Adopting a direct booking strategy is crucial for a rural hotel. By promoting the hotel's website and offering exclusive benefits to direct bookers, rural hotels can minimize distribution costs and maximize profit margins. Social media platforms can also be utilized as distribution channels, allowing rural hotels to engage with potential guests directly and offer personalized promotions. Implementing customer relationship management (CRM) systems can help rural hotels track guest preferences and behaviors, enabling targeted marketing campaigns and personalized offerings. By implementing channel management strategies such as diversifying distribution channels, implementing rate parity, utilizing revenue management systems, adopting a direct booking strategy, and leveraging social media and CRM systems, rural hotels can optimize revenue and maximize profitability.

VII. PROMOTIONS AND PACKAGES

In order to maximize revenue, rural hotels must strategically utilize promotions and packages. By offering promotional deals, hotels can attract new customers and incentivize them to book their stay. Promotions can take various forms, such as discounts on room rates, complimentary amenities or services, or special packages that combine multiple offerings. These incentives can be targeted towards specific segments of the market, such as families, couples, or business travelers, in order to increase their appeal. It is important for hotels to carefully plan and execute their promotions to ensure that they are cost-effective and align with the hotel's overall revenue management strategy. This includes considering factors such as the target market's preferences and purchasing behaviors, the hotel's revenue goals, and the seasonality or demand patterns in the rural area. Hotels should monitor the performance and effectiveness of their promotions through regular analysis of key performance indicators, such as booking rates and revenue generated. This will enable them to make data-driven decisions and make any necessary adjustments to their promotional strategies. Hotels can enhance the value of their offerings by creating attractive package deals that combine multiple services or amenities. This can not only increase the perceived value of the package but also encourage guests to book a longer stay or additional services. A rural hotel could create a package that includes a discounted room rate, complimentary breakfast, and a guided hiking tour in the nearby nature reserve. By bundling these offerings together and offering them at a discounted price, guests may feel that they are getting a better deal compared to booking each component separately. This can lead to increased bookings and revenue. Hotels should consider partnering with local attractions or businesses to create unique and exclusive packages that cannot be found elsewhere. This can help to differentiate the hotel from competitors and attract guests who are specifically seeking these experiences. Hotels should leverage technology and online booking platforms to effectively promote and distribute their promotional deals and packages. By using targeted advertising, social media, and email marketing campaigns, hotels can reach their desired target market and generate interest and bookings. It is important for hotels to regularly review and update their promotional offerings to keep them fresh and relevant to changing market demands. This can include introducing seasonal promotions, creating limited-time offers, or responding to current trends or events. By continuously innovating and optimizing their promotional strategies, rural hotels can effectively capture the attention of potential guests, increase bookings, and maximize their revenue.

DESIGNING ATTRACTIVE PROMOTIONS AND PACKAGES FOR TARGET CUSTOMERS

Designing attractive promotions and packages for target customers is a crucial aspect of revenue management for a rural hotel. By creating enticing offers, hotels can increase their occupancy rates and generate more revenue. One effective strategy is to tailor promotions to specific customer segments. A hotel located near a popular hiking trail can create a promotion targeting outdoor enthusiasts by offering discounted rates and complimentary hiking maps. Creating packages that combine accommodation with local experiences can be highly appealing to travelers seeking unique and immersive experiences. A rural hotel could collaborate with nearby wineries to offer wine tasting packages, or partner with local tour operators to create adventure packages that include activities such as kayaking or horseback riding. Another effective approach is to leverage special events or holidays to create limited-time promotions. By offering exclusive discounts or added amenities during these periods, hotels can create a sense of urgency and entice potential guests to book. It is essential to regularly evaluate and refine promotions based on customer feedback and market trends. Gathering feedback through guest surveys or online reviews can provide valuable insights into the preferences and expectations of target customers. This information can then be used to make necessary adjustments to promotions, ensuring they remain attractive and relevant. Monitoring market trends and analyzing competitors' promotions can provide valuable benchmarking information and help hotels stay ahead of the competition. It is important to promote promotions effectively through various marketing channels. Utilizing social media platforms, email marketing, and targeted online advertisements can reach a wide audience and generate interest in the hotel's offerings. Collaborating with travel agents or online travel agencies can also be beneficial in reaching a larger customer base. Designing attractive promotions and packages is an essential component of revenue management for rural hotels. By tailoring promotions to specific customer segments, creating unique packages, leveraging special events, gathering customer feedback, and utilizing effective marketing channels, hotels can attract and retain target customers, ultimately increasing their revenue and occupancy rates.

OFFERING VALUE-ADDED SERVICES TO ENHANCE CUSTOMER EXPERIENCE

Offering value-added services is another effective strategy to enhance customer experience and increase revenue for a rural hotel. By providing additional services that go above and beyond the basic accommodations, hotels can differentiate themselves from competitors and attract more customers. These value-added services can include complimentary breakfast, airport shuttle services, spa treatments, or entertainment options such as live music or storytelling sessions. By incorporating these services into their offerings, hotels not only enhance customer satisfaction but also create opportunities for additional revenue streams. A hotel can charge for premium breakfast options or offer special packages that include spa treatments. Value-added services can help to build a loyal customer base. When customers have a positive experience and receive added value during their stay, they are more likely to return and become repeat customers. This not only generates repeat business but also increases the likelihood of positive word-of-mouth recommendations, leading to referrals and new customers. Value-added services can also help to incentivize customers to book directly with the hotel rather than through a third-party website. By offering exclusive perks or benefits to direct bookers, hotels can encourage customers to bypass online travel agencies and make direct reservations instead. This not only reduces commission fees but also allows hotels to establish a direct relationship with their customers, enabling more personalized communication and targeted marketing efforts. Offering value-added services is a strategic approach to enhance customer experience, generate additional revenue, and build customer loyalty for rural hotels. By going above and beyond basic accommodations and providing special services or amenities, hotels can differentiate themselves, attract and retain customers, and create opportunities for additional revenue sources.

MONITORING THE EFFECTIVENESS OF PROMOTIONS AND ADJUSTING AS NEEDED

To ensure the success of promotions and optimize revenue, it is crucial for a rural hotel to monitor their effectiveness and make adjustments as needed. Monitoring the effectiveness of promotions involves tracking key performance indicators (KPIs) such as occupancy rate, average daily rate (ADR), and revenue per available room (RevPAR). By comparing these metrics before and after the implementation of promotions, hotel managers can assess whether the promotional activities have achieved their intended goals. In addition to quantitative metrics, hotel managers should also consider guest feedback and satisfaction scores to gauge the impact of promotions on the overall guest experience. Guest feedback can provide valuable insights into areas that need improvement or areas where promotions should be expanded. It is essential for hotel managers to stay informed about market trends and competitor activities by conducting regular market research. This will help them identify emerging opportunities or potential threats and adjust their promotional strategies accordingly. If a competitor hotel launches a new promotion targeting the same customer segment, the rural hotel may need to reassess its promotional offers to remain competitive. Advances in technology have made it easier to monitor and analyze the effectiveness of promotions. Hotel management systems and analytics tools can provide real-time data on occupancy, guest demographics, booking patterns, and revenue. By leveraging these technologies, hotel managers can gain valuable insights and make data-driven decisions about promotional activities. Continuous monitoring is instrumental in identifying trends or patterns in guest behavior that can inform promotional strategies. If the data shows that the hotel experiences a significant drop in occupancy during a particular month, the hotel can create targeted promotions during that period to attract more guests. Adjusting promotions based on the findings of monitoring efforts is equally important. Hotel managers should be prepared to modify or terminate promotions that do not yield the desired results. If a promotion fails to attract enough bookings or generate the expected revenue, it may be necessary to rethink the offer or explore alternative strategies. Conversely, if a promotion proves to be highly successful, hotel managers should consider extending or expanding it to capitalize on its popularity. Adjustments may be necessary due to external factors such as changes in market conditions, customer preferences, or economic factors. By regularly evaluating the effectiveness of promotions and making necessary adjustments, rural hotels can maximize their revenue potential and maintain a competitive edge in the market. Monitoring and adjusting promotions is an ongoing process that requires a proactive and data-driven approach. With the right tools and strategies in place, rural hotels can effectively evaluate the impact of promotions and fine-tune their marketing efforts to drive revenue growth.

VIII. CUSTOMER RELATIONSHIP MANAGEMENT

By focusing on building and maintaining strong relationships with customers, hotels can increase customer loyalty and ultimately drive revenue growth. One key aspect of customer relationship management is understanding the unique needs and preferences of individual guests. By collecting and analyzing data on customer behavior, hotels can personalize the guest experience, offering tailored promotions, services, and recommendations. This personalized approach not only increases customer satisfaction and loyalty but also enhances the hotel's ability to upsell and cross-sell to existing customers. Customer relationship management enables hotels to effectively communicate with guests through various channels, including email, social media, and mobile apps. By staying connected with customers and providing timely and relevant information, hotels can keep their brand top-of-mind, encourage repeat bookings, and attract new customers through positive word-of-mouth. Customer relationship management systems can help hotels track and manage customer feedback and resolve any issues or complaints promptly. This proactive approach to customer service not only improves the overall guest experience but also helps hotels identify trends and areas for improvement. Customer relationship management facilitates the collection and analysis of data on customer lifetime value and spending patterns. By identifying high-value customers and understanding their preferences, hotels can segment their customer base and target their marketing efforts more effectively. This targeted approach allows hotels to allocate resources wisely and maximize return on investment. Customer relationship management is essential for revenue management in a rural hotel. By focusing on building strong relationships with customers, personalizing the guest experience, and effectively communicating with guests, hotels can increase customer loyalty, drive revenue growth, and ultimately achieve long-term success.

IMPLEMENTING A CUSTOMER DATABASE TO TRACK GUEST PREFERENCES

Implementing a customer database for customer preference tracking is a crucial step in revenue management for a rural hotel. The hotel can gather valuable information about the preferences habits of its guests and past experiences By having access to a comprehensive customer database. This data can be used to personalize the stay of the guests and tailor promotions to meet their specific needs thereby increasing their overall quality and increasing their chance of returning to the next. Moreover the hotel can analyze customer behavior patterns and trends helping them make data-driven decisions about pricing inventory management and marketing strategies. For example if the database reveals that a specific segment of guests prefers certain amenities or activities the hotel can allocate resources accordingly to these preferences leading to a higher guest satisfaction and potentially greater revenue generation. The installation of a customer database will allow the hotel to communicate effectively with its guests. The hotel can stay connected to guests even after their stay Through personalized emails newsletters or targeted advertising campaigns fostering long-term relationships and encouraging repeat visits. The hotel can further enhance its customer database utilizing the information stored there this creates a sense of appreciation and loyalty among its customerele. This can be done by loyalty programs exclusive promotions or special rewards designed specifically for returning guests. Such personalized approaches demonstrate the hotel's commitment to satisfying its guests' needs and fostering a positive and memorable experience. The implementation of a customer database can also facilitate efficient decision-making processes for the hotel's revenue management team. By analyzing the data collected, the team can generate insights on market demand, stay preferences, and booking patterns. This information enables the team to optimize pricing strategies, manage room inventory effectively, and allocate resources efficiently. The data can be used to evaluate the success of different revenue management strategies, identify areas of improvement, and implement adjustments accordingly. These data-driven decisions aid in maximizing the hotel's revenue potential and enhancing its financial performance. Implementing a customer database to track guest preferences is an essential aspect of revenue management for rural hotels. By leveraging the information stored in the database, the hotel can personalize guest experiences, make data-driven decisions, establish better communication channels, reward loyal customers, and facilitate efficient decision-making processes. The implementation of a customer database is a valuable tool that can contribute to the overall success and sustainability of a rural hotel.

UTILIZING CUSTOMER SEGMENTATION TO PERSONALIZE OFFERS AND PRICING

Utilizing customer segmentation to personalize offers and pricing is a crucial strategy in revenue management for a rural hotel. By categorizing customers based on their preferences, behaviors, and demographics, hotels can tailor their offerings and pricing to suit individual needs. A hotel may divide customers into segments like business travelers, families, couples, and leisure tourists. By doing so, the hotel can then create targeted promotions and packages that appeal to the specific desires and interests of each segment. Business travelers may value amenities such as conference rooms and high-speed internet, while families may prioritize spacious rooms and child-friendly activities. By understanding these preferences, hotels can deliver personalized offers that enhance the overall guest experience and increase satisfaction. Pricing can also be customized based on segmentation. Offering discounts or special rates to certain segments during off-peak periods, for instance, can help attract more customers and increase occupancy rates. On the other hand, charging premium prices for high-demand segments can help maximize revenue during peak seasons. The insights gained from segmentation analysis can also assist hotels in forecasting demand patterns and making informed pricing decisions. By understanding the price sensitivity of each segment, hotels can optimize their revenue potential by charging the right prices to the right customers. Customer segmentation can help hotels identify loyal and high-value customers, leading to targeted loyalty programs and rewards. By tracking the preferences and

69

booking history of their guests, hotels can proactively offer personalized promotions and incentives to encourage repeat bookings. By recognizing and rewarding loyalty, hotels can foster long-term relationships with their most valuable customers and increase customer retention rates. Customer segmentation can play a vital role in attracting new customers. By analyzing the characteristics and preferences of potential segments, hotels can identify untapped markets and develop targeted marketing campaigns to reach these audiences. If the hotel identifies a growing trend of adventure-seeking tourists in the area, they can create adventure packages and tailor their marketing efforts to attract this specific segment. By catering to the unique needs and desires of various market segments, hotels can differentiate themselves from competitors and position themselves as the preferred choice for specific customer groups. Customer segmentation is a powerful tool in revenue management for a rural hotel. By understanding the diverse needs and preferences of customers, hotels can create personalized offers and pricing strategies that enhance the guest experience and maximize revenue potential. From tailored promotions and packages to customized pricing and loyalty programs, customer segmentation enables hotels to deliver targeted offerings that attract and retain customers. Segmentation analysis can assist in forecasting demand patterns and making informed pricing decisions, contributing to the hotel's overall revenue optimization. With its ability to identify untapped markets and differentiate the hotel from competitors, customer segmentation is an essential aspect of revenue management in the rural hotel industry.

BUILDING CUSTOMER LOYALTY THROUGH PERSONALIZED COMMUNICATION

In today's highly competitive market, where consumers have numerous options to choose from, it is essential for rural hotels to go the extra mile to make their guests feel valued and appreciated. One effective way to achieve this is through personalized communication. By tailoring their communication to the specific needs and preferences of individual guests, rural hotels can create a unique and memorable experience that fosters loyalty and encourages repeat visits. Personalized communication can take many forms, such as personalized email campaigns, customized offers, and tailored recommendations. These methods not only show that the hotel is attentive to the guest's needs but also help build a deeper connection and trust between the hotel and the guest. Personalized communication can also include proactive engagement, where the hotel reaches out to guests before and after their stay to ensure that their experience is outstanding. Such proactive communication can involve sending pre-arrival emails with relevant information about the hotel's amenities, local attractions, and any special events happening during the guest's stay. This not only helps in setting the right expectations but also allows the hotel to gather important preferences and requirements that can be used to personalize the guest's experience. Personalized communication can extend beyond the guest's stay by sending follow-up emails thanking the guest for their visit and requesting feedback on their experience. This not only shows appreciation but also provides an opportunity to address any concerns or issues the guest may have. All these personalized communication efforts contribute to building a strong emotional connection with the guest, making them feel like a valued part of the hotel's community. Rural hotels can use technology to enhance their personalized communication efforts. Using guest data collected through a customer relationship management (CRM) system, the hotel can offer customized promotions and exclusive offers based on the guest's preferences and past interactions with the hotel. By leveraging technology in this way, rural hotels can not only streamline their personalized communication efforts but also deliver a more seamless and convenient experience for their guests. Building customer loyalty through personalized communication is a powerful strategy for rural hotels to differentiate themselves from the competition and cultivate long-term relationships with their guests. By tailoring their communication to individual guests, proactively engaging with them, and leveraging technology, rural hotels can create a personalized experience that makes their guests feel valued and appreciated. This type of personalized communication fosters loyalty and encourages repeat visits, ultimately leading to increased revenue and success for the hotel.

IX. REVENUE MANAGEMENT SYSTEMS

With the constant fluctuation in demand and the need to max-imize revenue, hotels must invest in effective revenue manage-ment systems. These systems use data analytics and forecasting algorithms to determine the optimal pricing and inventory allo-cation strategies. By analyzing historical data, such as occu-pancy rates and pricing information, revenue management sys-tems can predict future demand and suggest appropriate pric-ing strategies. This helps hotels to optimize their room rates, ensuring that they are not leaving money on the table during peak periods while still attracting customers during low-de-mand periods. Revenue management systems allow hotels to segment their market and offer customized pricing and promo-tions to different customer segments. By tailoring their pricing strategies to specific target markets, hotels can attract more customers and increase their overall revenue. These systems also provide real-time inventory information, allowing hotels to monitor their availability and adjust their pricing accordingly. By implementing revenue management systems, hotels can effec-tively manage their supply and demand dynamics, ultimately maximizing their revenue potential. It is important to note that revenue management systems are not a one-size-fits-all solu-tion. Each hotel is unique, with its own set of challenges and market dynamics, so it is crucial to select a system that aligns with the hotel's specific needs and requirements. A comprehen-sive revenue management system should not only offer robust forecasting and pricing capabilities but also integrate with other hotel management systems, such as property management systems and online distribution channels. Seamless integration between these systems enables hotels to streamline their operations and ensure accurate pricing and inventory management across all channels. Hotels should also consider the scalability and adaptability of the revenue management system. As the business grows and market conditions change, the system should be able to accommodate these changes and continue to provide accurate and actionable insights. It is also worth mentioning that while revenue management systems can provide valuable data and insights, human expertise and decision-making remain essential in the process. Hotel revenue managers and their teams play a critical role in analyzing and interpreting the system's recommendations, as well as making strategic decisions based on their industry knowledge and intuition. Regular monitoring and evaluation of the system's performance are necessary to identify any areas for improvement and to ensure that the system is aligned with the hotel's overall revenue management strategy. By continuously refining and optimizing the revenue management system, hotels can stay competitive in the market and successfully navigate the ever-changing dynamics of the hotel industry. Revenue management systems are invaluable tools for hotels seeking to maximize their revenue potential. These systems offer data-driven insights, enabling hotels to optimize their pricing and inventory strategies based on demand fluctuations. By effectively managing their revenue, hotels can not only improve their financial performance but also enhance customer satisfaction and loyalty. Investing in a robust and tailored revenue management system is crucial for the success and growth of any hotel.

IMPLEMENTING A REVENUE MANAGEMENT SYSTEM TO AUTOMATE PROCESSES

One way in which a revenue management system can automate processes is through the integration of reservation and booking systems. By using a revenue management system, a hotel can streamline its reservation process by automatically updating availability and rates across all booking platforms. This eliminates the need for manual updates and reduces the risk of overbooking or listing incorrect rates. A revenue management system can automate the pricing process by analyzing market demand, competitor rates, and historical data to determine optimal pricing strategies. This eliminates the need for manual rate adjustments and ensures that a hotel's pricing is always competitive and tailored to current market conditions. A revenue management system can automate the forecasting process by analyzing and predicting demand patterns based on historical data. This helps hoteliers anticipate periods of high demand and adjust rates accordingly to maximize revenue. A revenue management system can automate the reporting process by generating real-time reports on key performance indicators such as occupancy rates, average daily rates, and revenue per available room. This provides hoteliers with valuable insights into their business performance and allows them to make data-driven decisions to optimize revenue. Implementing a revenue management system can greatly benefit a rural hotel by automating processes such as reservation, pricing, forecasting, and reporting. By automating these processes, a hotel can increase efficiency, reduce the risk of errors, and make data-driven decision.

76

UTILIZING DATA ANALYTICS TO MAKE INFORMED PRICING DECISIONS

The collection and analysis of relevant data can provide valuable insights into customer behavior, market trends, and competitor pricing strategies. By leveraging these insights, hotel management can adjust their pricing strategies in real-time to maximize revenue and profit. Data analytics can help identify patterns in customer demand, such as peak seasons or popular booking dates, allowing the hotel to implement dynamic pricing strategies to capture higher room rates during periods of high demand. Data analytics can help monitor and respond to changes in market conditions. By continuously tracking competitor pricing and market trends, the hotel can strategically position itself to offer competitive rates and packages that attract and retain customers. Data analytics can assist in identifying pricing inefficiencies and potential revenue leakage. By analyzing booking patterns and customer preferences, the hotel can identify opportunities to optimize its pricing structure, such as offering targeted discounts or adjusting room rates based on seasonal demand. This level of data-driven decision-making enables the hotel to make adjustments proactively rather than reactively, ensuring it remains competitive in the market. The utilization of data analytics in revenue management for a rural hotel is crucial in making informed pricing decisions. By leveraging data insights, the hotel can optimize its pricing strategies, respond to market changes, and identify potential revenue leakage. With the help of data analytics, the hotel can achieve its revenue and profit objectives, while also improving customer satisfaction by offering competitive rates and strategic pricing packages. This demonstrates the evolving nature of revenue management and the importance of utilizing data analytics in the hospitality industry. With the continued advancements in technology and the growing availability of data, the incorporation of data analytics will only become more essential for rural hotels as they aim to maximize revenue and achieve long-term success in a competitive market.

INTEGRATING REVENUE MANAGEMENT SYSTEM WITH OTHER HOTEL SYSTEMS

One way to achieve this integration is by connecting the revenue management system with the property management system (PMS). By doing so, information such as reservations, availability, and room rates can be easily synchronized, allowing for real-time updates and accurate inventory management. This integration also enables the revenue management system to have access to guest data, allowing for targeted marketing efforts and personalized pricing strategies. Another important system to integrate with the revenue management system is the central reservation system (CRS). Having seamless communication between the two systems ensures that all distribution channels are updated simultaneously with the most current rates and availability, minimizing the risk of overbooking or underselling. Integrating the revenue management system with the customer relationship management (CRM) system can further enhance the hotel's revenue management capabilities. By combining data from both systems, hotels can develop a comprehensive understanding of their customers' preferences and behaviors, enabling them to tailor their marketing strategies and pricing decisions accordingly. Integrating the revenue management system with the point of sale (POS) system allows for real-time tracking of revenue and expenses. This integration provides valuable insights into the profitability of various revenue streams, allowing managers to make informed decisions regarding pricing, discounts, and promotions. Integrating the revenue management system with the business intelligence (BI) system can provide valuable data analytics and reporting capabilities. The integration allows for the analysis of historical data, performance trends, and market demand, facilitating forecasting and decision-making processes. By merging these systems, hotels can derive meaningful insights into market conditions, customer behavior, and revenue opportunities, ultimately driving revenue growth and increasing profitability. Integrating the revenue management system with other hotel systems is vital for optimizing revenue and enhancing operational efficiency. By connecting the revenue management system with the PMS, CRS, CRM, POS, and BI systems, hotels can synchronize data, automate processes, and gain valuable insights into their customers, markets, and operations. This integration enhances inventory management, streamlines distribution channels, personalizes pricing strategies, tracks revenue and expenses, and provides valuable data analytics. A well-integrated revenue management system contributes to revenue growth and increased profitability for the hotel.

X. STAFF TRAINING AND EDUCATION

The employees of a hotel are the ones who interact directly with guests and have the power to influence their experience. It is essential that the staff is well-trained in revenue management principles and techniques. By educating the staff about revenue management strategies, they can better understand the importance of maximizing revenue and provide optimal service to guests. Training programs can include topics such as rate optimization, inventory management, and forecasting techniques. In addition to theoretical knowledge, practical training should also be included to allow staff members to apply revenue management concepts in real-life scenarios. This can be done through role-playing exercises or simulations. Ongoing education should be provided to ensure that staff members stay up to date with the latest developments in revenue management practices. This can be achieved through workshops, webinars, or industry conferences. When employees are well-trained and educated about revenue management, they become empowered to make informed decisions that positively impact the hotel's financial performance. They can identify opportunities to maximize revenue and take appropriate actions to capitalize on them. Well-trained staff can effectively communicate revenue management strategies to guests, helping them understand the value they are receiving and potentially upselling additional services or amenities. This not only generates additional revenue but also enhances the overall guest experience. Staff training and education contribute to a culture of continuous improvement within the hotel. By investing in the development of employees' revenue management skills, the hotel demonstrates its commitment to excellence and sets a high standard for performance. This culture of continuous improvement can motivate employees to actively seek out opportunities to enhance revenue and contribute to the hotel's success. Staff members who receive training and education in revenue management are more likely to be engaged and satisfied in their roles. They gain a sense of pride and accomplishment when they are able to apply their knowledge to drive revenue growth for the hotel. This, in turn, leads to improved employee retention, as satisfied employees are more likely to stay in their positions and contribute to the long-term success of the hotel. Staff training and education are critical components of a successful revenue management strategy for a rural hotel. By equipping employees with the necessary knowledge and skills, the hotel can maximize revenue potential and enhance guest satisfaction. Ongoing education ensures that staff members stay current with industry best practices and encourages a culture of continuous improvement. By investing in the development of staff members, hotels can create a team of empowered and motivated individuals who are committed to driving revenue growth and delivering exceptional service. Staff training and education are vital in achieving revenue management success for a rural hotel.

PROVIDING TRAINING ON REVENUE MANAGEMENT PRINCIPLES AND STRATEGIES

By offering training to hotel staff, particularly those involved in sales and marketing, the hotel can ensure that they have a thorough understanding of revenue management concepts and are equipped with the necessary skills to implement revenue management strategies effectively. Training can include topics such as demand forecasting, pricing optimization, distribution management, and effective use of technology tools. By imparting this knowledge to the staff, the hotel can improve their ability to identify potential revenue opportunities, make informed pricing decisions, and effectively manage demand fluctuations. Providing training on revenue management can help to foster a culture of revenue optimization within the hotel, encouraging all staff members to be mindful of revenue considerations in their day-to-day activities. This can lead to increased cooperation and coordination across different departments, ensuring that revenue management strategies are implemented consistently and effectively throughout the organization. Offering training on revenue management can also help to attract and retain qualified employees, as it demonstrates the hotel's commitment to professional development and provides employees with valuable skills that can enhance their careers in the hospitality industry. By providing training on revenue management principles and strategies, a rural hotel can equip its staff with the knowledge and skills necessary to optimize revenue and improve overall performance.

EMPOWERING STAFF TO MAKE REVENUE-RELATED DECISIONS

By giving staff the authority and knowledge to make decisions related to revenue, hotels can tap into their collective expertise and creativity. This empowerment can lead to a more dynamic and flexible approach to revenue management, allowing the hotel to adapt quickly to changing market conditions. When staff members feel trusted and valued, they are more likely to take ownership of their decisions and go the extra mile to generate revenue for the hotel. This can result in increased employee satisfaction and a higher level of engagement, both of which are important for maintaining a positive work environment and delivering exceptional guest experiences. Empowering staff to make revenue-related decisions can facilitate the delegation of tasks and responsibilities, easing the burden on management and creating a more efficient operation. This can free up managers to focus on strategic planning and analysis, rather than being bogged down in day-to-day decision-making. It is important to provide staff with the necessary training and guidance to ensure they have the skills and knowledge needed to make informed revenue decisions. This can include training sessions, workshops, and ongoing support and feedback. By investing in staff development, hotels can equip their employees with the tools they need to make effective revenue decisions and contribute to the overall success of the hotel. Regular communication and collaboration between staff members and management can help to foster a culture of shared responsibility and teamwork. This can create a positive and inclusive work environment where staff feel empowered and motivated to contribute to the hotel's revenue goals. Empowering staff to make revenue-related decisions is a valuable strategy for effective revenue management in rural hotels. Not only does it tap into the expertise and creativity of staff members, but it also improves employee satisfaction and engagement. By delegating decision-making authority, managers can focus on strategic planning and analysis, leading to more efficient operations. It is important to provide staff with the necessary training and support to ensure they have the skills and knowledge needed to make informed decisions. Regular communication and collaboration between staff and management can further enhance the effectiveness of this approach and foster a culture of shared responsibility. Empowering staff to make revenue-related decisions can ultimately contribute to the overall success and profitability of a rural hotel.

MONITORING STAFF PERFORMANCE AND PROVIDING FEEDBACK

By monitoring staff performance, hotel managers can identify areas where improvement is needed and take appropriate actions to address them. Regular performance evaluations can help to assess the strengths and weaknesses of each employee, allowing managers to focus on areas for improvement and provide targeted feedback. This feedback is essential for employee growth and development, as it not only highlights areas where they excel but also provides guidance on how they can enhance their performance in areas that need improvement. By providing clear and constructive feedback, managers can motivate their staff to take the necessary steps to enhance their skills and meet the hotel's revenue goals. Regular feedback sessions allow managers to provide recognition and appreciation for a job well done, boosting employee morale and creating a positive work environment. This, in turn, contributes to improved staff performance and customer satisfaction. Consistent monitoring and feedback also enable managers to identify training needs and opportunities for professional development. By identifying skill gaps, managers can arrange relevant training programs or seminars to equip staff with the necessary knowledge and skills to excel in their roles. By investing in ongoing staff development, rural hotels can ensure that their employees are up-to-date with industry trends and best practices, putting them in a better position to drive revenue growth. Another benefit of monitoring staff performance and providing feedback is that it helps in identifying and addressing any issues that may be hindering

87

employees' performance. By regularly reviewing performance data and metrics, managers can identify any performance issues or obstacles that need to be addressed promptly. This could include addressing concerns related to workload, workflow, equipment, or resources. By promptly addressing these issues, managers can ensure that employees have the necessary support and resources to perform their duties effectively and efficiently. By addressing performance issues in a timely manner, managers can prevent them from escalating and negatively impacting the hotel's revenue and reputation. Monitoring staff performance and providing feedback is an essential component of revenue management in rural hotels. By consistently evaluating performance, providing constructive feedback, and addressing any obstacles, managers can motivate and empower their staff to achieve optimal performance. This, in turn, contributes to improved customer satisfaction, increased revenue, and the hotel's overall success. Rural hotel managers should prioritize the regular monitoring of staff performance and invest in ongoing training and development to ensure that their employees are equipped with the necessary skills and support to drive revenue growth in a competitive market.

XI. TECHNOLOGY AND TOOLS

In the modern age, technological advancements have revolutionized every aspect of the hospitality industry, including revenue management for rural hotels. Technology has provided rural hotels with an array of tools and platforms to streamline their operations, enhance the guest experience, and maximize revenue. One such tool is the use of Property Management Systems (PMS). PMS allows hotels to automate various functions such as reservations, check-ins, check-outs, and billing processes. This automation not only saves time but also reduces the chances of human error, ensuring more efficient and accurate management of hotel operations. PMS provides data analytics capabilities, allowing hoteliers to track key performance indicators (KPIs) such as occupancy rates, revenue per available room (RevPAR), and average daily rate (ADR). This data-driven approach enables rural hotel managers to make informed decisions, optimize pricing strategies, and identify opportunities to increase revenue. Alongside PMS, online distribution channels such as Online Travel Agencies (OTAs) have also become invaluable tools for rural hotels. OTAs connect hotels with a broad customer base, facilitating easy access to potential guests from all around the world. These platforms provide hotels with a global reach, allowing them to attract guests who may have otherwise been unaware of their existence. OTAs often offer user-friendly interfaces, seamless bookings, and secure payment systems, providing guests with a hassle-free experience. Revenue management systems (RMS) have emerged as an essential tool for rural hoteliers to optimize their pricing strategies. RMS employ sophisticated algorithms to analyze market demand, competitor rates, and historical data to recommend optimal room rates and inventory allocations. This real-time pricing intelligence ensures that rural hotels remain competitive and maximize revenue potential. Customer relationship management (CRM) systems have allowed rural hotels to develop more personalized and targeted marketing strategies. CRM maintains a database of guest information, preferences, and behaviors, allowing hotels to tailor their marketing efforts and deliver customized promotions and offers to their target audience. By effectively utilizing CRM, rural hotels can enhance guest loyalty, increase repeat business, and boost revenue. The rise of social media platforms cannot be ignored when discussing technology and tools in revenue management for rural hotels. Social media has opened up new avenues for hotels to engage with and attract guests. Hotels can leverage these platforms to showcase their offerings, share guest testimonials, and promote local attractions. Social media allows for direct communication with guests, enabling hotels to address queries, resolve issues, and provide personalized recommendations. By consistently maintaining an active presence on social media, rural hotels can build brand awareness, foster customer engagement, and ultimately drive revenue growth. Technology has significantly transformed revenue management for rural hotels. The advent of tools such as PMS, OTAs, RMS, CRM, and social media platforms has empowered rural hoteliers to optimize their operations, enhance the guest experience, and maximize revenue potential. It is imperative for rural hotels to

embrace these advancements and adapt to the changing landscape to stay competitive in the industry.

UTILIZING REVENUE MANAGEMENT SOFTWARE FOR DATA ANALYSIS

Utilizing revenue management software for data analysis offers a plethora of benefits to rural hotels. Revenue management software allows hoteliers to gather and analyze vast amounts of data, enabling them to make more informed decisions about pricing and inventory management. The software aggregates data from various sources, such as customer booking patterns, competitor rates, and market demand, providing valuable insights for effective revenue maximization. By examining historical and real-time data, hoteliers can identify trends and patterns, allowing them to forecast demand accurately. This enables them to strategize pricing to optimize revenue and occupancy levels while remaining competitive within the marketplace. Revenue management software helps rural hotels monitor and evaluate performance metrics, such as average daily rate, revenue per available room, and occupancy rate. Analyzing these metrics helps hoteliers to identify underperforming periods and take proactive measures to improve revenue generation. Revenue management software provides detailed reports and visual representations of data, making it easier for hoteliers to interpret and communicate insights to stakeholders. These reports can help inform revenue management strategies, highlighting areas of improvement and opportunities for growth. Revenue management software often integrates with other hotel management systems, such as property management software and online distribution channels. This integration streamlines operations and facilitates seamless data flow across different platforms, reducing the risk of errors and saving time. With accurate and up-to-date data, rural hotels can make more informed decisions regarding pricing adjustments and promotional campaigns. Revenue management software enables hotels to implement dynamic pricing strategies, which involve adjusting rates in real-time based on market demand and competitor activity. This flexibility allows rural hotels to capitalize on fluctuations in demand and optimize revenue during high-demand periods, such as holidays or events, while offering attractive deals during low-demand periods. Utilizing revenue management software for data analysis empowers rural hotels to make data-driven decisions, enhance their revenue generation capabilities, and remain competitive in an ever-evolving hospitality industry.

IMPLEMENTING ONLINE BOOKING SYSTEMS FOR SEAMLESS RESERVATIONS

Implementing online booking systems for seamless reservations is a critical step for rural hotels looking to improve their revenue management strategies. With the increasing popularity of online travel agencies such as Expedia and Booking. com, having a strong online presence is essential for attracting guests. By adopting an online booking system, hoteliers can streamline the reservation process, making it convenient and efficient for both guests and staff. Online booking systems offer numerous benefits, including 24/7 accessibility, which allows potential guests to make reservations at any time, regardless of their location or time zone. These systems can provide real-time availability and pricing information, enabling guests to make informed decisions. Integrating online booking systems with a hotel's website and social media platforms can enhance its visibility and reach potential guests who may otherwise not have considered staying in a rural location. The implementation of online booking systems also helps hotels in efficiently managing their inventory by automating the reservation process. As a result, hoteliers can optimize their room utilization, minimize the risk of overbooking, and ensure that each booking is accurately entered into the system. These systems can generate valuable data and analytics that can assist hotels in making data-driven revenue management decisions. By analyzing trends in booking patterns, occupancy rates, and pricing, hoteliers can adjust their strategies to maximize revenue and profitability. Online booking systems can be integrated with other revenue management tools, such as dynamic pricing software, to offer personalized pricing to guests based on factors such as demand, seasonality, and customer segments. The implementation of online booking systems also opens up opportunities for targeted marketing and promotional campaigns. By capturing guests' contact information during the reservation process, hotels can send personalized emails or offers to guests, encouraging repeat bookings and fostering loyalty. By leveraging online reviews and ratings from satisfied guests, hotels can enhance their reputation and attract new customers. It is crucial for rural hotels to carefully select an online booking system that aligns with their specific needs and budget. Factors such as ease of use, integration capabilities, customer support, and cost should be considered when choosing a system. Hoteliers must ensure that their online booking system complies with security and data protection regulations to safeguard guest information. Implementing online booking systems is a crucial step for rural hotels to enhance their revenue management strategies and remain competitive in the modern hospitality industry. These systems offer numerous benefits, including seamless reservations, improved guest convenience, increased visibility, optimized inventory management, valuable data analytics, and targeted marketing opportunities. By carefully selecting and integrating an online booking system, rural hotels can streamline their operations, enhance the guest experience, and maximize their revenue potential.

USING REVENUE MANAGEMENT DASHBOARDS FOR REAL-TIME INSIGHTS

Revenue management dashboards are an essential tool for hotels to gain real-time insights into their revenue performance. These dashboards provide a comprehensive view of the hotel's revenue data, allowing managers to make informed decisions and optimize their revenue strategies. By analyzing key metrics such as occupancy rates, average daily rates, and revenue per available room, hotel managers can identify trends and patterns and adjust their pricing and inventory strategies accordingly. Revenue management dashboards allow managers to track and evaluate the effectiveness of their marketing campaigns and promotional activities. By monitoring the performance of different channels and segments, hotels can allocate their resources more effectively and invest in initiatives that generate the highest returns. Real-time insights provided by revenue management dashboards enable hotels to respond swiftly to changes in market conditions and customer demand. By continuously monitoring their revenue data, hotel managers can quickly identify any fluctuations in demand and adjust their pricing and availability to maximize revenue potential. This proactive approach can help hotels stay competitive in a dynamic market and avoid missed revenue opportunities. Revenue management dashboards can also assist hotels in identifying potential revenue leakage and optimizing their pricing structures. By analyzing data on rate integrity and rate parity, hotel managers can identify any inconsistencies or disparities in their pricing across different channels and take corrective actions. This not only helps hotels maintain a consistent pricing strategy but also ensures that they are not losing revenue due to undercutting or overpricing. Revenue management dashboards can provide valuable insights into customer preferences and booking patterns. By analyzing data on guest demographics, previous booking behavior, and length of stay, hotels can tailor their offerings and promotions to specific customer segments, thereby enhancing guest satisfaction and driving repeat business. Revenue management dashboards can integrate data from various sources such as online travel agencies, global distribution systems, and property management systems. By consolidating data from different channels and platforms into a single dashboard, hotels can centralize their revenue management processes and make more accurate and timely decisions. This also allows for better collaboration and communication among different departments, ensuring that everyone has access to the same real-time information. Revenue management dashboards provide hotels with real-time insights into their revenue performance, enabling managers to make informed decisions and optimize their revenue strategies. By analyzing key metrics, monitoring market conditions, and identifying potential revenue leakage, hotels can increase their revenue potential and stay competitive in a dynamic market. Revenue management dashboards help hotels respond swiftly to changes in customer demand and tailor their offerings to specific customer segments. By integrating data from different sources, these dashboards enable hotels to centralize their revenue management processes and enhance collaboration among different departments. Revenue management dashboards are a powerful tool that can drive revenue growth and improve the overall financial performance of a hotel.

XII. MONITORING AND EVALUATION

Through monitoring, the hotel can keep track of its performance, identify areas of improvement, and make informed decisions based on data. This involves the collection and analysis of various key performance indicators, such as room occupancy rate, average daily rate, revenue per available room, and total revenue generated. By monitoring these indicators regularly, the hotel can assess its current revenue performance and compare it to desired goals and benchmarks. Monitoring enables the identification of emerging trends and patterns that may impact the hotel's revenue, such as seasonality, market demand, or customer preferences. This information is essential for the hotel to adapt and adjust its revenue management strategies accordingly. Evaluation, on the other hand, involves the continuous assessment of the effectiveness and efficiency of revenue management practices. It entails analyzing the results achieved through revenue management strategies and evaluating their impact on the hotel's financial performance. This includes assessing the return on investment for different revenue management initiatives, analyzing the effectiveness of pricing strategies, and evaluating the success of promotional campaigns. Evaluation also involves comparing the hotel's performance to industry benchmarks and competitors to identify areas where the hotel can improve and stay competitive. By rigorously evaluating revenue management practices, the hotel can identify strengths and weaknesses, make informed decisions, and implement changes that will optimize revenue generation. To effectively monitor and evaluate revenue management, the hotel must have the necessary systems and tools in place. This includes implementing a robust revenue management system that collects and consolidates data from various sources. This system should provide comprehensive reports and analytics that allow the hotel to easily analyze key performance indicators and track progress over time. The hotel should employ skilled personnel who can proficiently interpret the data and provide actionable insights. Regular training and professional development for revenue management staff are crucial to ensure they have the necessary skills and knowledge to analyze and interpret data accurately. The hotel should establish a system for regular performance reviews and feedback sessions to address any issues or challenges promptly. This allows for continuous improvement and refinement of revenue management strategies. Monitoring and evaluation are essential components of revenue management for a rural hotel. By regularly monitoring key performance indicators, the hotel can make informed decisions based on data and identify areas of improvement. Evaluation enables the assessment of the effectiveness and efficiency of revenue management practices and provides insights into the hotel's financial performance. To effectively monitor and evaluate revenue management, the hotel must have the right systems and tools in place, as well as skilled personnel. By implementing a robust monitoring and evaluation process, the hotel can optimize its revenue generation and stay competitive in the market.

TRACKING KEY PERFORMANCE INDICATORS TO MEASURE REVENUE PERFORMANCE

Key performance indicators (KPIs) provide valuable insights into the financial health and success of a hotel by quantifying key metrics that influence revenue generation. By monitoring KPIs on a regular basis, hoteliers can identify trends, evaluate performance, and make informed strategic decisions to enhance revenue outcomes. One important KPI to consider is the average daily rate (ADR), which represents the average revenue generated per occupied room. A higher ADR indicates that guests are willing to pay more for their stay, resulting in increased revenue for the hotel. Another significant KPI is the revenue per available room (RevPAR), which measures the hotel's efficiency in utilizing its available room inventory to generate revenue. A higher RevPAR signals that the hotel is maximizing its revenue potential and effectively managing its inventory. The occupancy rate is a critical KPI that indicates the percentage of available rooms that are filled over a given period. A higher occupancy rate implies greater demand, leading to increased revenue for the hotel. The average length of stay (LOS) is an important metric to track, as it directly impacts revenue performance. A longer LOS typically results in higher revenue, as guests are staying for extended periods and generating more revenue per stay. The reservation cancellation rate should be monitored as it can affect revenue performance. A higher cancellation rate indicates potential revenue loss due to last-minute cancellations, necessitating proactive measures to minimize cancellations and maximize revenue. Another vital KPI to track is the revenue generated from ancillary services, such as food and beverage, spa, and events. By monitoring revenue generated from these sources, hoteliers can identify areas of opportunity for upselling and cross-selling, further driving revenue growth. The cost per occupied room (CPOR) is a crucial KPI to measure the financial efficiency of the hotel. By calculating the costs associated with serving each occupied room, hoteliers can evaluate the profitability of their operations and take necessary actions to optimize cost management. Tracking key performance indicators is imperative for measuring revenue performance in the hospitality industry. KPIs such as ADR, RevPAR, occupancy rate, LOS, reservation cancellation rate, revenue from ancillary services, and CPOR provide valuable insights into the financial health and success of a hotel. By regularly monitoring these metrics, hoteliers can identify areas of improvement, make informed strategic decisions, and ultimately enhance revenue outcomes.

CONDUCTING REGULAR REVENUE REVIEWS AND ANALYSIS

By regularly reviewing and analyzing revenue data, hotel managers can gain valuable insights into the performance of their revenue strategies, identify areas for improvement, and make data-driven decisions to optimize revenue. Performing regular revenue reviews allows hotels to track their revenue performance over time and identify trends and patterns that can help them better understand their market and customer behavior. Analysis of revenue data can also reveal opportunities for revenue growth, such as identifying high-demand periods or popular services that can be further capitalized on. Conducting revenue analysis enables hotels to identify any revenue leaks or inefficiencies in their operations, such as pricing discrepancies or underutilized assets. By addressing these issues, hotels can maximize their revenue potential and increase their profitability. Regular revenue reviews provide hotels with insights into their competitors' pricing strategies and market positioning, allowing them to adjust their own pricing strategies accordingly. This information can be invaluable for rural hotels, as they often face unique challenges due to their location and competition. Conducting regular revenue reviews and analysis facilitates collaboration and communication among different departments within the hotel, as revenue data is often collected from various sources. This shared knowledge enables all team members to understand the hotel's revenue goals and work collaboratively towards achieving them. Revenue reviews can also help identify any gaps in staff training or skills that may be inhibiting revenue performance. By addressing these gaps, hotels can improve their overall revenue strategy and ensure that all employees are aligned towards the same revenue goals. Conducting regular revenue analysis allows hotels to monitor the effectiveness of any revenue management tools or technologies they have implemented. By evaluating the impact of these tools on revenue performance, hotels can make informed decisions about their use and potential investments in other revenue management solutions. Conducting regular revenue reviews and analysis is essential for rural hotels to effectively manage their revenue. Such reviews provide valuable insights into the hotel's revenue performance, identify areas for improvement, and facilitate data-driven decision-making. By analyzing revenue data, hotels can optimize their revenue strategies, increase profitability, and stay competitive in their market. Revenue reviews encourage collaboration and communication among different departments within the hotel, address employee training needs, and evaluate the effectiveness of revenue management tools. Regular revenue reviews and analysis play a crucial role in revenue management for rural hotels and should be a consistent practice for sustainable revenue growth.

MAKING ADJUSTMENTS TO REVENUE MANAGEMENT STRATEGIES BASED ON EVALUATION RESULTS

Making adjustments to revenue management strategies based on evaluation results is a crucial step in ensuring the effectiveness and success of a revenue management system. By regularly evaluating the performance of the revenue management strategies implemented, hotel managers can identify areas of improvement and make necessary adjustments to enhance revenue generation. One important aspect of evaluation is examining the revenue data and analyzing the key metrics such as average daily rate, occupancy rate, and revenue per available room. These metrics provide insights into the effectiveness of pricing and inventory management strategies. If the average daily rate is lower than desired, it may indicate the need for adjusting pricing strategies to attract more customers. If the occupancy rate is consistently high or low, it may signify a need for reevaluating inventory management practices. Evaluating the performance of revenue management strategies also involves monitoring the effectiveness of distribution channels. This includes analyzing the performance of online travel agencies, direct bookings, and other channels. By comparing and contrasting the performance of different distribution channels, hotel managers can identify the channels that generate the highest revenue and allocate resources accordingly. If a particular online travel agency consistently yields low revenue, the hotel may decide to decrease its reliance on that channel and focus on more profitable channels. Evaluation results can also shed light on the impact of external factors on revenue management strategies. By analyzing the revenue data during peak seasons versus off-peak seasons, hotel managers can assess the effectiveness of pricing strategies during different periods. This information can guide them in making adjustments to pricing strategies to maximize revenue during peak seasons and maintain profitability during off-peak seasons. Evaluation results can highlight the impact of marketing initiatives on revenue generation. By analyzing the revenue data before and after implementing a marketing campaign, hotel managers can determine whether the campaign was successful in attracting more customers and increasing revenue. Adjustments to revenue management strategies based on evaluation results should be an iterative process. Hotel managers should continuously evaluate the performance of revenue management strategies and make necessary adjustments to stay responsive to changing market conditions. This may involve conducting regular revenue meetings to bring together key stakeholders and discuss the evaluation results. By involving key team members, such as revenue managers, sales managers, and marketing managers, hotel managers can benefit from diverse perspectives and expertise. This collaborative approach ensures that adjustments are well-informed and well-executed. It is important to document and track the results of adjustments made to revenue management strategies. This allows hotel managers to learn from past experiences and determine the effectiveness of previous adjustments. By maintaining a record of adjustments and their impact on revenue generation, hotel managers can build a knowledge base that informs future decision-making processes. Making adjustments to revenue management strategies based on evaluation results is an ongoing process that is vital for the success of a revenue management system. By evaluating key metrics, monitoring distribution channels, considering external factors, and involving key team members, hotel managers can make informed adjustments to enhance revenue generation. This iterative process ensures that revenue management strategies remain responsive to market conditions and maximize profitability.

XIII. COLLABORATION WITH LOCAL BUSINESSES

By partnering with local businesses, such as restaurants, tour operators, and souvenir shops, the hotel can offer its guests a comprehensive and tailored experience. The hotel can collaborate with a nearby restaurant to offer special dining packages that include a discounted meal for guests. This not only benefits the hotel by generating additional revenue through the partnership, but also enhances the overall experience for guests as they can enjoy local cuisine without having to venture far from the hotel. Partnering with tour operators allows the hotel to offer excursions and activities to its guests, which not only enhances their stay but also generates revenue through commissions or referral fees. By collaborating with local businesses, the hotel can tap into the expertise and resources of these entities, creating a win-win situation for all parties involved. The hotel is able to provide its guests with a unique and authentic experience, while the local businesses benefit from increased exposure and potentially higher sales. Collaboration with local businesses can also lead to increased customer loyalty and repeat business. When guests are satisfied with the services and experiences provided by the hotel, they are more likely to return in the future and recommend the property to others. This word-of-mouth marketing can be incredibly valuable for a rural hotel looking to attract more guests and increase its revenue. Collaborating with local businesses can also help the hotel build strong relationships within the community. By supporting local enterprises, the hotel becomes an integral part of the local economy and fosters goodwill among residents. This can lead to further opportunities for collaboration, such as hosting community events or participating in local tourism initiatives. By working together with local businesses, the hotel can create a thriving ecosystem that benefits not only the property but also the entire community. Revenue management for a rural hotel goes beyond traditional revenue optimization techniques. It requires a holistic approach that encompasses pricing strategies, segmentation, distribution, and collaboration with local businesses. By implementing these strategies effectively, a rural hotel can maximize its revenue potential and create a unique and memorable experience for its guests. Revenue management is not just about making more money, but about providing value to guests and creating sustainable growth for the hotel.

ESTABLISHING PARTNERSHIPS WITH LOCAL ATTRACTIONS AND BUSINESSES

By creating alliances with nearby tourist attractions and local businesses, the hotel can tap into a wider customer base and offer unique experiences to guests. Collaborating with local museums, historical sites, or outdoor activity providers can create opportunities for package deals and exclusive offers, thereby attracting more visitors to the hotel. Through these partnerships, the hotel can also negotiate discounted rates or special promotions, which can be leveraged to increase occupancy rates during periods of low demand. Partnering with local businesses such as restaurants, wineries, or specialty stores can enhance the hotel's overall guest experience by providing convenient amenities or additional services. Offering vouchers for a complimentary wine tasting at a nearby vineyard can incentivize guests to choose the rural hotel over competitors. Establishing partnerships with local businesses can lead to cross-promotional opportunities, where each partner can promote the other's offerings to their respective customer bases, generating more visibility and potential bookings. These collaborations not only bolster the rural hotel's bottom line but also contribute to the local economy by fostering community engagement and supporting the growth of neighboring businesses. Establishing partnerships with local attractions and businesses is a strategic approach that not only diversifies the hotel's revenue streams but also enriches the guest experience and fosters economic growth in the rural area.

CREATING JOINT PROMOTIONS AND PACKAGES TO ATTRACT MORE CUSTOMERS

Joint promotions and packages are a valuable strategy for attracting more customers to a rural hotel. By partnering with local businesses or attractions, the hotel can create enticing offers that cater to a variety of interests. The hotel could collaborate with a nearby spa to offer a discounted weekend package that includes a one-night stay and a spa treatment. This joint promotion not only appeals to individuals looking for a relaxing getaway but also allows the hotel to tap into the spa's existing customer base. The hotel could partner with a popular outdoor activity provider to offer adventure packages, which could include activities such as hiking, kayaking, and zip-lining. By bundling these activities with a hotel stay, the hotel can attract outdoor enthusiasts who are seeking accommodations in the area. Joint promotions and packages not only provide added value for customers but also create a mutually beneficial partnership between the hotel and other local businesses. By collaborating with partners, the hotel can expand its reach and increase its visibility in the market. This strategy can be particularly effective for a rural hotel that may struggle with low foot traffic and limited exposure. Joint promotions and packages can also allow the hotel to differentiate itself from competitors and create a unique selling proposition. By offering unique, customized experiences, the hotel can stand out in an overcrowded marketplace and attract customers who are looking for something different. The hotel could collaborate with a nearby winery to create a wine tasting package, which includes a guided tour of the vineyard, a tasting session, and a bottle of wine upon check-in. This type of package not only appeals to wine enthusiasts but also provides an immersive experience that guests will remember and share with others. Joint promotions and packages are a valuable tool for attracting more customers to a rural hotel. By collaborating with local businesses or attractions, the hotel can create enticing offers that cater to a variety of interests. This strategy not only provides added value for customers but also allows the hotel to tap into new markets and increase its visibility. By offering unique and customized experiences, the hotel can differentiate itself from competitors and create a memorable stay for guests. Joint promotions and packages can play a crucial role in driving revenue and ensuring the long-term success of a rural hotel.

LEVERAGING LOCAL EVENTS AND FESTIVALS TO INCREASE HOTEL REVENUE

One effective strategy for increasing hotel revenue in a rural area is to leverage local events and festivals. Rural areas often have a variety of unique events and festivals that draw visitors from near and far. By capitalizing on these events, hotels can increase their occupancy rates and overall revenue. A hotel located near a popular music festival can offer special packages and promotions specifically targeted to festival attendees. This could include discounted room rates, complimentary transportation to and from the festival grounds, and exclusive access to after-parties or events. By offering these enticing incentives, hotels are able to attract festival-goers and generate additional revenue. Hotels can partner with event organizers to provide accommodations for performers, staff, and attendees, further increasing their customer base. Hotels can create special packages for other local events such as agricultural fairs, sporting tournaments, or cultural festivals. These packages can include discounted rates, tickets to event activities, and even guided tours of the area. By creating these tailored packages, hotels are able to appeal to a specific target market and position themselves as the preferred accommodation option for event attendees. Hotels can also take advantage of off-peak periods by hosting their own exclusive events or seminars. By hosting events during quieter times, hotels can attract visitors who may not have otherwise considered staying in the area. A hotel located near a vineyard could host wine tasting events or workshops during weekdays to attract wine enthusiasts who are looking for a unique experience. This not only increases revenue but also helps to promote the hotel as a destination in itself. Partnering with local businesses and attractions can also help hotels leverage local events and festivals. By developing strategic partnerships, hotels can offer guests exclusive discounts or access to nearby attractions or activities. A hotel located near a hiking trail could collaborate with a local adventure company to provide discounted adventure packages to hotel guests. This not only enhances the guest experience but also encourages visitors to extend their stay and explore the local area. Leveraging local events and festivals can be an effective strategy for increasing hotel revenue in rural areas. By creating tailored packages, hosting their own events, and partnering with local businesses, hotels can tap into the influx of visitors attending these events and create a unique and compelling experience for their guests. The key lies in understanding the target market, identifying the most appealing events, and developing enticing offers and promotions that set the hotel apart from the competition.

XIV. SUSTAINABLE REVENUE MANAGEMENT PRACTICES

These practices involve implementing strategies that not only maximize revenue in the short term but also respect and preserve the natural environment and local community. One such practice is the adoption of energy-efficient systems within the hotel. This includes using LED lights, installing motion sensor switches, and utilizing renewable energy sources such as solar panels. These measures not only reduce energy consumption and carbon footprint but also lead to cost savings for the hotel. Another sustainable revenue management practice is promoting eco-friendly tourism. This involves offering packages that highlight the natural beauty and cultural heritage of the surrounding area, encouraging guests to engage in activities that have a minimal impact on the environment. By partnering with local tour operators and emphasizing responsible travel, the hotel can attract environmentally conscious guests and forge stronger connections with the local community. Implementing waste management practices can contribute to the sustainability of the hotel. This includes reducing, reusing, and recycling waste generated by both guests and staff. A thorough waste separation program can lead to cost savings through reduced landfill fees and the potential sale of recyclable materials. A sustainable revenue management practice that should not be overlooked is water conservation. By installing low-flow fixtures in guest rooms and implementing water-saving measures in laundry and kitchen facilities, the hotel can significantly reduce its water consumption. Educating and incentivizing guests to participate in water-saving practices, such as reusing towels and taking shorter showers, can further contribute to sustainability efforts. Implementing smart pricing strategies can also be considered a sustainable revenue management practice. By using dynamic pricing algorithms, the hotel can adjust its rates based on demand and availability, maximizing revenue without overbooking rooms. This not only increases profitability but also ensures a responsible and fair distribution of resources. The implementation of sustainable revenue management practices also includes supporting the local economy. This can be achieved by sourcing local products and services whenever possible, thereby reducing the carbon footprint associated with transportation and supporting local businesses. It is important to establish partnerships with local farmers and artisans, promoting their products to hotel guests and creating economic opportunities within the community. Sustainable revenue management practices are indispensable for a rural hotel's success and long-term viability. By integrating energy-efficient systems, promoting eco-friendly tourism, implementing waste management practices, conserving water, practicing smart pricing, and supporting the local economy, the hotel can achieve a balance between financial profitability and responsible environmental and social stewardship. These practices not only lead to increased revenue but also contribute to the preservation of the natural environment, the well-being of the local community, and the overall sustainability of the business.

INCORPORATING SUSTAINABILITY INITIATIVES INTO REVENUE MANAGEMENT STRATEGIES

By integrating environmentally responsible practices, such as energy conservation, waste reduction, and water management, hotels can not only contribute to the preservation of the environment but also attract a growing number of socially conscious travelers. Implementing sustainability initiatives can offer a competitive advantage by differentiating the hotel from others in the market. The use of energy-efficient appliances and renewable energy sources can significantly reduce operational costs, resulting in long-term financial savings. By reducing waste and implementing recycling programs, hotels can demonstrate their commitment to sustainability and appeal to environmentally conscious guests. By incorporating sustainable practices into their revenue management strategies, rural hotels can not only positively impact the environment but also enhance their profitability and appeal to a broader customer base.

PROMOTING ECO-FRIENDLY PRACTICES TO ATTRACT ENVIRONMENTALLY CONSCIOUS GUESTS

By implementing sustainable practices, such as using renewable energy sources, recycling programs, and reducing waste, hotels can demonstrate their commitment to environmental stewardship. One way to promote these practices is by providing information to guests about the hotel's sustainable initiatives. Hotels can collaborate with local environmental organizations to hold workshops or events that educate guests on the importance of eco-friendly practices. Showcasing certifications, such as LEED (Leadership in Energy and Environmental Design), can further enhance the hotel's appeal to environmentally conscious guests. These certifications assure guests that the hotel meets high standards of sustainability. Another strategy to promote eco-friendly practices is by offering incentives for guests to engage in sustainable behaviors, such as discounted rates for using public transportation or offering eco-friendly amenities. With the growing awareness and concern for the environment, many travelers seek out accommodations that align with their values. Promoting eco-friendly practices not only attracts environmentally conscious guests but also positions the rural hotel as a socially responsible and forward-thinking establishment. By implementing these strategies, hotel managers can tap into a niche market of environmentally conscious guests, increasing the hotel's revenue while also contributing to the preservation of the environment.

MONITORING AND REDUCING WASTAGE TO IMPROVE COST EFFICIENCY

By closely monitoring wastage, hotel managers can identify areas where resources are being wasted, such as excessive energy usage, food spoilage, or overstocking of supplies. This allows them to take proactive measures, such as implementing energy-saving practices, optimizing inventory levels, and implementing waste reduction strategies. Hotels can invest in energy-efficient lighting and appliances, implement inventory management systems to better track and control stock levels, and train staff to reduce food waste through portion control and proper storage techniques. Hotel managers can also collaborate with suppliers to minimize packaging waste and explore environmentally friendly alternatives. By reducing wastage, hotels can not only improve cost efficiency but also contribute to environmental sustainability. Technology can play a vital role in monitoring and reducing wastage by providing real-time data on resource usage, allowing managers to identify patterns, spot trends, and make informed decisions. Smart meters can monitor energy consumption, while kitchen management systems can track food usage and waste. This data can be used to set targets, identify areas for improvement, and provide feedback to staff. Hotels can engage their guests in waste reduction efforts by promoting green practices and encouraging responsible consumption. This can be achieved through initiatives such as offering rewards for reducing energy usage, educating guests about recycling and waste management, and implementing towel and linen reuse programs. Such initiatives not only help reduce wastage but also enhance the overall guest experience by promoting a sustainable and responsible image. Monitoring and reducing wastage is vital for improving cost efficiency in revenue management for a rural hotel. By closely monitoring and addressing areas of wastage, hotel managers can identify opportunities for efficiency gains and cost savings. Implementing energy-saving practices, optimizing inventory levels, and reducing food and packaging waste are just some of the strategies that can be employed. In addition to cost savings, such measures can contribute to environmental sustainability and enhance the overall guest experience. Embracing technology and engaging guests in waste reduction efforts can further enhance the effectiveness of waste management initiatives. By making wastage reduction a priority, rural hotels can achieve cost-efficiency goals while aligning with environmentally responsible practices.

XV. CRISIS MANAGEMENT AND ADAPTABILITY

In today's dynamic and unpredictable business environment, being able to effectively handle crises and adapt to changing circumstances is essential for survival and success. The ability to anticipate potential crises, develop contingency plans, and respond promptly and decisively when unexpected situations arise can make a significant difference in minimizing the negative impact on operations and reputation. Being adaptable allows a rural hotel to stay flexible and responsive to the evolving needs and preferences of guests. This may involve constantly monitoring market trends, introducing new services and amenities, or adjusting pricing strategies accordingly. Crisis management and adaptability are not just reactive measures; they are proactive strategies that enable a rural hotel to thrive amidst uncertainty and competition. By proactively preparing for crises and being adaptable in responding to changes, a rural hotel can enhance its overall performance and maintain a competitive edge in the market.

DEVELOPING CONTINGENCY PLANS FOR UNEXPECTED EVENTS

In an industry that is highly vulnerable to external factors such as weather conditions, natural disasters, and economic fluctuations, being prepared for unexpected events can make a significant difference in a hotel's financial performance. One effective strategy for developing contingency plans is to conduct a risk assessment of potential threats specific to the hotel's location. By identifying and assessing potential risks, hotel management can determine the most appropriate actions to take in response to each scenario. These actions may include investing in insurance coverage, establishing emergency response protocols, or diversifying revenue streams to mitigate the impact of unexpected events. Hotels should develop strong relationships with local authorities and emergency services to facilitate efficient and effective communication during crisis situations. In the event of an unforeseen circumstance, having clear lines of communication can help hotel staff quickly implement contingency plans and minimize disruptions to operations. Hotels should establish a clear chain of command and designate specific roles and responsibilities for each staff member during emergency situations. By assigning clear roles and responsibilities, hotel management can ensure that all necessary actions are taken promptly and efficiently. Another important aspect of developing contingency plans is maintaining accurate and up-to-date records of hotel operations, including financial statements, reservation data, and guest information. These records can be invaluable in assessing the financial impact of unexpected events and facilitating the implementation of recovery plans. Regularly reviewing and updating these records can also help hotel management identify potential areas of improvement or vulnerability. In addition to these proactive measures, hotels should also consider the integration of technology solutions to enhance their ability to respond to unexpected events. Implementing an automated revenue management system can enable hotels to quickly adjust pricing and inventory in response to changing market conditions, ensuring that revenue is maximized even during challenging circumstances. Hotels should regularly review and revise their contingency plans to take into account any changes in the external environment or internal operations. As the hospitality industry is constantly evolving, hotels must remain flexible and adaptable to ensure their contingency plans remain relevant and effective. Developing contingency plans for unexpected events is essential for a rural hotel's revenue management. By conducting risk assessments, establishing communication channels with local authorities, assigning clear roles and responsibilities, maintaining accurate records, integrating technology solutions, and regularly reviewing and updating plans, hotels can effectively respond to unexpected events and minimize negative financial impacts. Hotels that prioritize contingency planning are better prepared to weather unforeseen circumstances, ensuring their long-term success in a volatile industry.

ADAPTING REVENUE MANAGEMENT STRATEGIES DURING CRISES OR LOW-DEMAND PERIODS

During crises or low-demand periods, it is crucial for hotels to adapt their revenue management strategies in order to navigate the challenges that arise. In these situations, hotels must be proactive in identifying and implementing cost-saving measures. One strategy is to reevaluate staffing needs and adjust employee schedules accordingly. By assessing the occupancy levels and predicted demand, hotels can make informed decisions about the number of staff members required to adequately serve guests. This allows for a reduction in labor costs without compromising the quality of service provided. Hotels can explore opportunities to collaborate with local businesses or offer package deals to attract more customers. Partnering with nearby tourist attractions or restaurants to offer discounted rates or bundled packages can entice guests to choose their property over competitors. Hotels can strategically adjust their pricing strategies during low-demand periods. Implementing dynamic pricing strategies, such as offering lower rates for extended stays or last-minute bookings, can help to stimulate demand and attract price-sensitive customers. It is also important for hotels to leverage technology and utilize online platforms to optimize their revenue management during crises or periods of low demand. By monitoring the competitive landscape, hotels can adjust their rates in real-time to stay competitive in the market. Investing in digital marketing strategies, such as search engine optimization and targeted social media campaigns, can help hotels reach a wider audience and generate more bookings. Hotels can consider diversifying their revenue streams during low-demand periods. This could include offering additional services, such as hosting conferences or events, partnering with local businesses for corporate retreats, or offering specialized packages for specific target markets, such as wellness retreats or outdoor adventure packages. By expanding their product offerings, hotels can attract a wider range of guests and generate additional revenue. It is crucial for hotels to optimize their inventory management during crises or low demand periods. By closely monitoring demand patterns and adjusting inventory allocation accordingly, hotels can maximize revenue potential. This includes implementing strategies such as length-of-stay controls, overbooking, or releasing early bird rates to encourage bookings. Effective revenue management systems and technology can provide the necessary tools and data to make informed decisions regarding inventory allocation. During crises or low-demand periods, it is imperative for hotels to adapt their revenue management strategies to remain competitive and financially sustainable. By implementing cost-saving measures, collaborating with local businesses, adjusting pricing strategies, leveraging technology, diversifying revenue streams, and optimizing inventory management, hotels can navigate these challenging periods and position themselves for long-term success.

IMPLEMENTING FLEXIBLE CANCELLATION AND REFUND POLICIES

With unpredictable demand patterns and a fluctuating customer base, providing flexibility in canceling and refunding reservations can attract more bookings and enhance customer satisfaction. By allowing guests to cancel or modify their reservations without penalty within a certain timeframe, hotels can provide peace of mind and a sense of control to customers, leading to increased trust and loyalty. Offering refunds for canceled reservations can help minimize revenue loss as guests may be more likely to rebook in the future or recommend the hotel to others. It is important to strike a balance between flexibility and the hotel's financial stability. By setting reasonable cancellation deadlines and considering factors like seasonality and occupancy levels, the hotel can ensure that its cancellation and refund policies are fair and sustainable. Implementing technology solutions, such as automated cancellation policies and online refund processing, can streamline the process and reduce administrative costs. This not only improves operational efficiency but also enables hotels to provide faster and more convenient service to guests. Effective communication of the cancellation and refund policies is crucial. Clear and transparent information should be provided on the hotel's website and booking platforms, as well as during the reservation process. This can help guests make informed decisions and prevent any potential misunderstandings or disputes. Regularly reviewing and refining the cancellation and refund policies based on guest feedback and market trends is also essential. By analyzing cancellations and refunds patterns, the hotel can identify potential areas for improvement and optimize its revenue management strategies. Implementing flexible cancellation and refund policies can have a significant impact on the revenue and reputation of a rural hotel. By providing flexibility and convenience to guests, hotels can enhance customer satisfaction and loyalty. By setting reasonable deadlines and leveraging technology, hotels can ensure that their cancellation and refund policies are fair and sustainable. Effective communication of these policies and continuous monitoring and refinement are also critical for success. By embracing flexibility in cancellations and refunds, rural hotels can navigate the challenges of demand fluctuations while maximizing revenue and delivering exceptional guest experiences.

XVI. FEEDBACK AND REVIEWS

When guests take the time to share their experiences and opinions, it provides valuable insight into the strengths and weaknesses of the hotel. Customers often leave reviews on various online platforms, such as TripAdvisor or Google Reviews, which prospective guests rely on when making their booking decisions. Positive reviews can act as endorsements and attract new guests to the rural hotel, while negative reviews can have the opposite effect, deterring potential visitors. It is essential for the hotel management to actively monitor and respond to reviews, whether positive or negative, to show that they value their guests' feedback. Responding to positive reviews by expressing gratitude and acknowledging the guests' satisfaction can further reinforce customer loyalty. Addressing negative reviews promptly and professionally is crucial in demonstrating the hotel's commitment to resolving issues and improving the guest experience. By understanding the specific areas that need improvement, the management can make targeted adjustments to enhance guest satisfaction. Feedback and reviews not only inform potential guests but also provide essential guidance to the hotel management in shaping their revenue management strategies.

ENCOURAGING GUESTS TO PROVIDE FEEDBACK AND REVIEWS

By actively seeking feedback, hotel management can gauge customer satisfaction and identify areas of improvement. This feedback also serves as valuable marketing material, as positive reviews and testimonials can attract potential guests. To encourage guests to provide feedback, hotels can offer incentives such as discounts or complimentary services. Providing guests with an easy and convenient platform to leave reviews, such as an online survey or a guestbook in each room, can increase the likelihood of receiving feedback. It is essential for hotel staff to actively seek out feedback from guests during their stay, as this allows the staff to address any issues or concerns immediately, improving the overall guest experience. Responding promptly and courteously to guest feedback demonstrates a commitment to customer satisfaction and can help build customer loyalty. Encouraging guest feedback and reviews is a continuous and ongoing process that requires proactive efforts from hotel staff. By actively seeking guest feedback, hotels can stay informed about their customers' experiences and make necessary improvements to enhance guest satisfaction and maximize revenue.

136

MONITORING ONLINE REVIEWS AND ADDRESSING GUEST CONCERNS PROMPTLY

In today's digital age, potential guests rely heavily on online reviews to make decisions about where to stay. Negative reviews can significantly impact a hotel's reputation and ultimately affect its revenue. It is imperative for hotels to closely monitor online review platforms and social media channels to stay informed about guests' experiences. Addressing any concerns or issues raised by guests promptly is equally important. By responding to negative reviews and addressing guest concerns, hotels demonstrate their commitment to customer satisfaction and show that they value feedback from their guests. This not only helps to mitigate any potential damage caused by negative reviews but also allows the hotel to improve its services and exceed guest expectations. It is essential for hotels to respond to all online reviews, regardless of whether they are positive or negative. By acknowledging positive reviews, hotels can show their appreciation for guest feedback and foster a positive relationship with their guests. Responding to negative reviews shows potential guests that the hotel is proactive in resolving issues and is genuinely concerned about the satisfaction of its guests. It is important for hotel management to understand that addressing guest concerns promptly is not just about issuing a standard apology; it requires active engagement and a genuine desire to resolve any issues. When responding to negative reviews, hotels should apologize for any shortcomings and offer a solution or compensation where appropriate. By taking ownership of the situation and offering a resolution, hotels can demonstrate their willingness to rectify any issues and turn a negative experience into a positive one. Addressing guest concerns promptly can help hotels identify patterns or recurring issues that may need to be addressed within the organization. By analyzing the feedback received from guests, hotels can identify areas of improvement and implement necessary changes to enhance the overall guest experience. This continuous feedback loop allows hotels to stay connected with their guests and adapt their practices to meet ever-changing guest expectations. To effectively monitor online reviews and address guest concerns promptly, hotels can utilize various tools and technologies. Social listening tools can help hotels stay informed about online conversations related to their property, allowing for timely responses and proactive engagement. Hotels can establish clear protocols and allocate resources to ensure that guest feedback is promptly addressed. This may involve assigning dedicated staff members to monitor online review platforms and social media channels and providing them with the authority to address guest concerns in a timely manner. By prioritizing the prompt resolution of guest concerns, hotels can demonstrate their commitment to excellent customer service and increase their chances of receiving positive reviews and repeat business. Monitoring online reviews and addressing guest concerns promptly are critical components of revenue management for a rural hotel. By actively engaging with guest feedback and striving for continuous improvement, hotels can enhance their reputation, attract more guests, and ultimately increase their revenue.

UTILIZING POSITIVE REVIEWS TO ATTRACT MORE CUSTOMERS

Nowadays, online reviews have become increasingly influential in consumers' decision-making process. Positive reviews act as a form of social proof, giving potential customers trust and confidence in the hotel's quality and service. When a rural hotel has a large number of positive reviews, it creates a positive reputation for the establishment. This reputation can help to differentiate the hotel from competitors and increase its visibility in search engine results. Positive reviews can also enhance the hotel's online presence and improve its search engine ranking. Many potential customers rely on search engines when looking for accommodation options, and having a strong online presence can increase the hotel's visibility to these customers. Utilizing positive reviews strategically, such as featuring them prominently on the hotel's website or social media platforms, can help to showcase the hotel's strengths and attract more potential guests. Positive reviews can also be utilized as part of the hotel's marketing and promotional efforts. The hotel can create targeted advertising campaigns that highlight positive reviews and testimonials from satisfied guests. These campaigns can be run on platforms such as social media or email marketing to reach a wider audience. By leveraging the positive experiences of past guests, the hotel can effectively communicate the value and quality of its services to potential customers. Another way to utilize positive reviews is by integrating them into the hotel's customer service and staff training initiatives. By sharing positive reviews with staff members, they can see firsthand the impact their work has on guests' experiences and satisfaction. This can motivate the staff to continue providing excellent service and exceed guests' expectations. Customer feedback from positive reviews can be analyzed to identify areas of strength and areas for improvement. This information can be used to enhance the hotel's operations and deliver even better experiences to future guests. Utilizing positive reviews is a powerful strategy for attracting more customers to a rural hotel. Positive reviews act as social proof and help to build a positive reputation for the hotel. They can also enhance the hotel's online presence and improve its search engine ranking. By strategically featuring positive reviews on the hotel's website, social media platforms, and in marketing campaigns, the hotel can effectively communicate its value and quality to potential customers. Positive reviews can be utilized to motivate staff members and improve customer service. By leveraging the experiences of past guests and continuously improving based on customer feedback, a rural hotel can attract more customers and increase its revenue.

XVII. CONTINUOUS LEARNING AND IMPROVEMENT

Revenue management is an ever-evolving field, with new techniques, technologies, and trends constantly emerging. As such, it is important for revenue managers to stay updated with the latest developments in the industry. This can be done through attending conferences, participating in webinars, and staying connected with industry experts. By continuously learning and gaining new insights, revenue managers can effectively adapt their strategies and make informed decisions to maximize revenue and profitability. Continuous improvement is necessary to enhance revenue management practices. Revenue managers should regularly review and analyze their performance and identify areas for improvement. This could involve assessing the effectiveness of pricing strategies, evaluating the success of promotional campaigns, or exploring new distribution channels. By systematically evaluating their actions and outcomes, revenue managers can identify strengths and weaknesses, make necessary adjustments, and enhance their revenue management practices. Continuous learning and improvement also involve embracing feedback and learning from past mistakes. Revenue managers should actively seek feedback from customers, employees, and other stakeholders to gain insights into areas that may need improvement. This could be done through surveys, reviews, or even informal conversations. By listening to the perspectives of others, revenue managers can gain a deeper understanding of customer needs and preferences and identify opportunities to enhance the guest experience. Learning from past mistakes and failures is essential for continuous improvement. Revenue managers should adopt a culture of learning from setbacks and use them as opportunities for growth. By analyzing why certain strategies or actions did not yield the desired outcomes, revenue managers can identify potential pitfalls and develop strategies to overcome them. This reflective mindset ensures that revenue managers are constantly refining their approaches and avoiding repeating the same mistakes. Continuous learning and improvement in revenue management also involve staying updated with the latest technological advancements. Technology plays a crucial role in revenue management, with software and tools providing valuable insights and automation capabilities. Revenue managers should actively seek opportunities to enhance their technological proficiency, whether it is learning how to utilize revenue management software effectively or exploring emerging technologies such as artificial intelligence or machine learning. By harnessing the power of technology, revenue managers can streamline processes, improve accuracy, and gain a competitive edge. Continuous learning and improvement in revenue management are essential for rural hotels to thrive in a dynamic and competitive industry. By staying updated with industry developments, embracing feedback, learning from mistakes, and leveraging technology, revenue managers can enhance their revenue management practices, drive profitability, and deliver exceptional guest experiences. In a constantly evolving landscape, the ability to adapt and improve is what sets successful revenue managers apart, and it is a mindset that should be cultivated and nurtured in rural hotel.

STAYING UPDATED ON INDUSTRY TRENDS AND BEST PRACTICES

Staying updated on industry trends and best practices is crucial for success in any field, and this is especially true in the hospitality industry. With technology advancing rapidly and consumer preferences constantly changing, it is important for rural hotels to stay abreast of the latest developments in their sector. By staying updated on industry trends and best practices, rural hotels can ensure that they are offering the best possible experience to their guests and remaining competitive in their market. One way to stay updated is by attending industry conferences and trade shows, where hoteliers can learn about the latest trends, technological advancements, and best practices in revenue management. These conferences provide an opportunity to network with other industry professionals and gain insights into successful strategies that can be implemented in rural hotel settings. Hoteliers should regularly engage in professional development through online resources and industry publications. Subscribing to industry newsletters, reading industry blogs, and participating in webinars are all ways for rural hoteliers to stay informed about current trends and best practices. Joining professional organizations and associations can provide valuable networking opportunities and access to resources and information that can help rural hotels stay current and competitive. By participating in these organizations, rural hoteliers can connect with peers and experts in the field, share experiences and best practices, and stay updated on the latest industry developments. It is important for rural hotels to consistently monitor and analyze data from their own operations. This data can reveal important insights about guest booking patterns, revenue performance, and market trends. By regularly reviewing this data, rural hoteliers can identify areas for improvement, adapt their strategies to meet changing consumer demands, and make informed decisions about pricing, inventory management, and marketing efforts. Staying updated on industry trends and best practices is essential for rural hotels to thrive in today's competitive market. By attending conferences, engaging in professional development, joining professional organizations, and analyzing data, rural hoteliers can ensure that they are providing the best possible experience for their guests and staying ahead of the curve in their industry.

ATTENDING CONFERENCES AND WORKSHOPS ON REVENUE MANAGEMENT

By attending these events, hotel managers can gain valuable insights and knowledge from industry experts and experienced professionals. Conferences and workshops provide a platform for networking, allowing hoteliers to connect with other professionals in the field and learn from their experiences. These events often feature sessions and panel discussions where participants can learn about the latest trends, best practices, and innovative strategies in revenue management. Through these interactive sessions, hotel managers can acquire new ideas and techniques to optimize revenue in their specific rural hotel context. By staying up-to-date with the evolving revenue management landscape, attending conferences and workshops enables rural hoteliers to implement cutting-edge strategies and stay ahead of their competitors. Attending such events showcases the hotel's commitment to professional development and continuous learning, thereby enhancing its reputation and positioning it as a leader in revenue management practices. Conferences and workshops on revenue management offer a unique opportunity for rural hotels to learn, network, and gain valuable insights to optimize their revenue management processes.

SEEKING FEEDBACK FROM STAFF AND GUESTS TO IDENTIFY AREAS FOR IMPROVEMENT

To ensure continual improvement and provide the best possible experience for guests, it is essential for a rural hotel to seek feedback from both staff and guests. By actively seeking input, the hotel can identify areas in need of improvement and take appropriate action. Staff members, who have firsthand experience with daily operations, can provide valuable insights into potential areas for enhancement. They may notice inefficiencies in processes or identify ways to enhance guest satisfaction. By encouraging staff members to provide feedback, the hotel can tap into their expertise and foster a collaborative environment. Feedback from guests is crucial in understanding their perspective and identifying areas where the hotel may be falling short. Guests can offer valuable insight into their experience, highlighting both positive aspects and areas for improvement. By actively soliciting guest feedback, the hotel demonstrates its commitment to customer satisfaction and shows that it values guest opinions. This feedback can then be used to implement changes that address any concerns or make improvements that enhance the overall guest experience. Opening lines of communication and providing convenient avenues for feedback, such as comment cards or online surveys, can encourage guests to provide their input. Proactively seeking feedback helps the hotel stay ahead of potential problems or negative reviews. By addressing issues early on and taking steps to rectify any shortcomings, the hotel can effectively mitigate the risk of negative feedback. When guests notice that their feedback is being heard and taken into consideration, it fosters a sense of trust and loyalty towards the hotel. This can lead to positive word-of-mouth recommendations and repeat business, ultimately contributing to the hotel's overall revenue and success. Seeking feedback from staff and guests is crucial for a rural hotel to identify areas for improvement. By leveraging the expertise of staff members and actively soliciting guest opinions, the hotel can gain valuable insights into potential enhancements. This feedback can then be used to implement changes that address any concerns and enhance the overall guest experience. By proactively seeking feedback and demonstrating a commitment to customer satisfaction, the hotel can foster a sense of trust and loyalty among its guests, resulting in positive word-of-mouth recommendations and increased revenue.

XVIII. CONCLUSION

Revenue management is a critical strategy for the success of a rural hotel. By implementing effective revenue management techniques, rural hotels can maximize their revenue potential and improve their financial performance. The use of forecasting and demand analysis allows hotel managers to anticipate fluctuations in demand and adjust their pricing and availability accordingly. Inventory control systems enable hotels to optimize the number of rooms available for sale and minimize the risk of revenue loss due to overbooking or underbooking. The implementation of dynamic pricing strategies allows hotels to respond to changes in demand and market conditions in real-time, ensuring that room rates are always competitive and reflective of the value offered. Distribution management plays a key role in revenue management, as hotels must carefully select the distribution channels that will reach their target market and generate the most bookings. Through the use of online travel agencies, global distribution systems, and direct booking channels, hotels can expand their reach and increase their visibility to potential guests. It is crucial for rural hotels to continuously monitor and analyze their revenue performance to identify areas of improvement and make data-driven decisions. Through the use of key performance indicators and revenue management software, hotels can track their success and adjust their strategies as needed. Revenue management is an integral part of managing a rural hotel, allowing managers to optimize revenue, improve financial performance, and provide guests with a memorable experience. By implementing effective revenue management practices, rural hotels can increase their competitiveness in the market and achieve long-term sustainability.

RECAP OF REVENUE MANAGEMENT STRATEGIES FOR RURAL HOTELS

In summary, revenue management strategies play a crucial role in enhancing the profitability of rural hotels. Dynamic pricing, length of stay controls, and distribution management are key strategies that rural hotels can employ to optimize their revenue. Dynamic pricing allows hotels to adjust their room rates in real-time based on demand and market conditions. By implementing length of stay controls, hotels can incentivize guests to extend their stay or discourage short stays during peak periods. Effective distribution management involves carefully evaluating and selecting the most suitable distribution channels to reach a wider audience and maximize bookings. These strategies, when implemented together, can help rural hotels maximize their revenue potential and effectively compete in the market. It is important for rural hotel managers to continuously monitor and analyze market trends, stay updated on industry best practices, and adapt their revenue management strategies accordingly to achieve long-term success. By developing a comprehensive revenue management plan that incorporates these strategies, rural hotels can maintain a competitive edge and achieve sustainable growth in a highly competitive market.

IMPORTANCE OF IMPLEMENTING EFFECTIVE REVENUE MANAGEMENT PRACTICES

The implementation of effective revenue management practices is of utmost importance for any hotel, regardless of its location. Revenue management refers to the process of optimizing pricing, distribution, and marketing strategies to maximize revenue and overall profitability. In today's highly competitive hospitality industry, where customers have a plethora of options to choose from, hotels need to employ a strategic approach to revenue management to stay ahead. By implementing revenue management practices, hotels can capitalize on market demand, identify pricing opportunities, and make informed decisions about inventory allocation. These practices allow hotels to not only increase revenue but also effectively manage costs and improve the bottom line. Effective revenue management practices provide valuable insights into customers' preferences and booking patterns, enabling hotels to tailor their offerings and marketing strategies accordingly. This can lead to increased customer satisfaction and loyalty, as hotels are able to offer personalized experiences that meet the unique needs and expectations of their guests. Revenue management also plays a crucial role in optimizing revenue during periods of high demand or low demand. During peak seasons, hotels can capitalize on the strong demand by adjusting prices and optimizing pricing strategies to maximize revenue. On the other hand, during periods of low demand, hotels can implement dynamic pricing strategies, such as offering discounts or special promotions, to attract customers and fill up occupancy. The implementation of effective revenue management practices allows hotels to adapt to changing market conditions, maximize revenue, and remain competitive in the industry. In rural areas, where the number of potential customers may be limited, revenue management becomes even more crucial. By implementing revenue management practices, rural hotels can leverage their unique selling points, such as their location, natural beauty, or cultural attractions, to attract customers and achieve higher revenue. Effective revenue management practices in rural hotels can also help in bridging the gap between seasons of high and low demand. By carefully analyzing booking patterns and demand trends, rural hotels can strategically adjust their pricing and marketing strategies to attract customers during off-peak seasons. This not only helps in increasing revenue during slow periods but also ensures a more stable and sustainable business model for rural hotels. Effective revenue management practices in rural hotels can also lead to positive economic impact on the local community. As revenue increases, rural hotels have the potential to generate more jobs and contribute to local economic development. This can have a multiplier effect as increased employment opportunities will lead to higher income levels, increased spending, and further growth of the local economy. The implementation of effective revenue management practices is essential for hotels in both urban and rural areas. By optimizing pricing, distribution, and marketing strategies, hotels can increase revenue, improve profitability, and enhance customer satisfaction. In the case of rural hotels, revenue management becomes even more important as it allows them to capitalize on their unique advantages and bridge the gap between high and low demand periods. Effective revenue management practices in rural hotels can have a positive impact on the local community by generating employment opportunities and contributing to economic development. Hence, hotels must prioritize the implementation of effective revenue management practices to ensure long-term success in today's competitive hospitality industry.

POTENTIAL BENEFITS AND LONG-TERM SUCCESS FOR RURAL HOTELS

One potential benefit for rural hotels is the opportunity to attract a different type of traveler. Many urban hotels cater to business travelers or tourists who are looking for a convenient location in the heart of a city. In contrast, rural hotels can offer a unique experience for travelers who want to escape the hustle and bustle of urban life and immerse themselves in nature. This can include activities such as hiking, wildlife spotting, or simply enjoying the peace and quiet of a rural setting. By marketing themselves as a peaceful and rejuvenating retreat, rural hotels have the potential to attract travelers who are seeking a more relaxed and natural environment. Rural hotels can also tap into the growing trend of eco-tourism. Many travelers today are becoming more conscious of their impact on the environment and are actively seeking out accommodations that are sustainable and environmentally friendly. Rural hotels have the advantage of being located in natural surroundings, which presents opportunities for incorporating eco-friendly practices such as using renewable energy sources, implementing water conservation measures, and supporting local, organic, or farm-to-table food options. By promoting their commitment to sustainability and eco-tourism, rural hotels can appeal to a specific segment of travelers who prioritize environmental responsibility. In the long term, rural hotels have the potential for sustained success and growth. As more people yearn for a break from the noise and stress of urban life, rural destinations are becoming increasingly popular. The appeal of a peaceful and untouched natural environment can be a driving force for travelers looking to unwind and connect with nature. This demand for rural experiences provides rural hotels with the opportunity to establish themselves as key players in the tourism industry. To ensure long-term success, rural hotels must adapt to changing consumer demands and market trends. This can include offering unique experiences or activities that cannot be found in urban settings, such as guided nature walks, horseback riding, or stargazing tours. By continuously innovating and evolving to meet the needs of travelers, rural hotels can remain relevant and maintain a competitive edge in the market. Rural hotels can also forge partnerships with local businesses and attractions to create a comprehensive and appealing tourism package. A rural hotel may collaborate with nearby wineries, farms, or historical sites to offer visitors a diverse range of experiences during their stay. These partnerships not only provide additional revenue streams for the hotel but also enhance the overall guest experience. Rural hotels have the potential to benefit from their unique location and natural surroundings. They can attract a different type of traveler who is looking for a peaceful retreat and an eco-friendly experience. With the growing demand for rural experiences, rural hotels have the opportunity for sustained success and long-term growth. By adapting to changing consumer demands and forging partnerships with local businesses, rural hotels can position themselves as desirable destinations and create memorable experiences for their guests.

BIBLIOGRAPHY

Robison Wells. 'Feedback.' Harper Collins, 10/2/2012

James Svetec. 'Airbnb For Dummies.' Symon He, John Wiley & Sons, 3/10/2023

Eleftherios Thalassinos. 'Digital Transformation, Strategic Resilience, Cyber Security and Risk Management.' Simon Grima, Emerald Group Publishing, 9/28/2023

Trudi Bridges. 'Exploring Contingency Planning for Adverse Weather Conditions.' How Well Do Event Managers Plan for Inclement Weather? A Thesis Submitted in Partial Fulfilment of the Requirements for the Degree of Masters of Business (MBus), Unitec Institute of Technology, 1/1/2014

Djordje Cosic. 'Crisis Management.' Introducing Companies Organizational Reactivity and Flexibility, Mladen Pecujlija, Nova Science Publishers, Incorporated, 1/1/2019

Ana Laura Torres. 'Sustainability in Hospitality.' How Innovative Hotels are Transforming the Industry, Miguel Angel Gardetti, Routledge, 9/8/2017

Peter Nijkamp. 'Quantitative Methods in Tourism Economics.' Álvaro Matias, Springer Science & Business Media, 12/13/2012

Louise Hudson. 'Marketing for Tourism, Hospitality & Events.' A Global & Digital Approach, Simon Hudson, SAGE Publications, 12/4/2023

Clarence Harris. 'Planning a Wholesale Poultry Layout in a Multiple-occupancy Building.' Agricultural Research Service, U.S. Department of Agriculture, 1/1/1972

Melville Saayman. 'Collaboration in Tourism Businesses and Destinations.' A Handbook, Dogan Gursoy, Emerald Group Publishing, 1/29/2015

Policy and Global Affairs. 'STTR: An Assessment of the Small Business Technology Transfer Program.' National Academies of Sciences, Engineering, and Medicine, National Academies Press, 1/11/2016

Planners Collaborative, Inc. 'Elements Needed to Create High Ridership Transit Systems.' TranSystems Corporation, Transportation Research Board, 1/1/2007

Asian Development Bank. 'A Comparative Analysis of Tax Administration in Asia and the Pacific.' 2020 Edition, Asian Development Bank, 2/1/2020

Marcus Sheridan. 'They Ask, You Answer.' A Revolutionary Approach to Inbound Sales, Content Marketing, and Today's Digital Consumer, John Wiley & Sons, 8/6/2019

J. Bradley Cousins. 'Monitoring and Evaluation Training.' A Systematic Approach, Scott G. Chaplowe, SAGE Publications, 10/15/2015

Siti Nor Nadrah Muhamad. 'Research Exhibition in Mathematics and Computer Sciences (REMACS 6.0).' Nur Fatihah Fauzi, College of Computing, Informatics and Mathematics, 7/17/2023

Carol Ann Browne. 'Tools and Weapons.' The Promise and the Peril of the Digital Age, Brad Smith, Penguin, 9/10/2019

Michael Armstrong. 'Armstrong's Handbook of Performance Management.' An Evidence-Based Guide to Performance Leadership, Kogan Page Publishers, 1/3/2022

Thomas Potterfield. 'The Business of Employee Empowerment.' Democracy and Ideology in the Workplace, Bloomsbury Publishing USA, 3/30/1999

Malte Rücker. 'Revenue Management Integration.' GRIN Verlag, 2/1/2012

McKinsey Chief Marketing & Sales Officer Forum. 'Big Data, Analytics, and the Future of Marketing and Sales.' CreateSpace Independent Publishing Platform, 8/2/2014

Andreas Thams. 'Airline Revenue Management.' Current Practices and Future Directions, Curt Cramer, Springer Nature, 11/10/2021

Alessandro Capocchi. 'Economic Value and Revenue Management Systems.' An Integrated Business Management Model, Springer, 12/30/2018

Wolfgang Katsch. 'International E-Business – Building Online Customer Loyalty with Relationship Management.' GRIN Verlag, 11/7/2001

Cassandra Fenyk. 'AI Unleashed: Harnessing Artificial Intelligence to Start and Grow Your Business.' Fenyk Enterprises LLC, 5/15/2023

Jabaree Dunham-Carson. 'Conversations in Communication, Volume 2.' Customer Relationship Management (CRM) As a Function of Public Relations, Amazon Digital Services LLC - Kdp, 4/29/2015

Chuck West. 'The Manager's Guide to Distribution Channels.' Linda Gorchels, McGraw Hill Professional, 5/7/2004

Hamideh Afsarmanesh. 'Collaborative Networks of Cognitive Systems.' 19th IFIP WG 5.5 Working Conference on Virtual Enterprises, PRO-VE 2018, Cardiff, UK, September 17-19, 2018, Proceedings, Luis M. Camarinha-Matos, Springer, 9/6/2018

Khalid Hasan. 'Strategic Marketing Management in Asia.' Case Studies and Lessons across Industries, Syed Saad Andaleeb, Emerald Group Publishing, 12/22/2016

Gemma Hereter. 'Introduction to Revenue Management for Hotels.' Tools and Strategies to Maximize the Revenue of Your Property, CreateSpace Independent Publishing Platform, 1/17/2017

Mark Simpson. 'The Book Direct Playbook.' Say Goodbye to OTAs with Proven Marketing Tactics to Boost Direct Bookings, Boostly, 1/1/2022

Julian Dent. 'Distribution Channels.' Understanding and Managing Channels to Market, Kogan Page Publishers, 6/3/2011

Ajay Das. 'An Introduction to Operations Management.' The Joy of Operations, Routledge, 12/22/2015

Mohamad Y. Jaber. 'Inventory Management.' Non-Classical Views, CRC Press, 8/11/2009

Charles W. Chase. 'Demand-Driven Forecasting.' A Structured Approach to Forecasting, John Wiley & Sons, 7/16/2013

Ger Koole. 'An Introduction to Business Analytics.' Lulu.com, 1/1/2019

Enno Siemsen. 'Demand Forecasting for Managers.' Stephan Kolassa, Business Expert Press, 8/17/2016

Sabine Kuester. 'EBOOK: Marketing Management.' Christian Homburg, McGraw Hill, 12/16/2012

Robert Phillips. 'Pricing and Revenue Optimization.' Stanford University Press, 8/5/2005

Tim J. Smith. 'Pricing Strategy.' Setting Price Levels, Managing Price Discounts, & Establishing Price Structures, South-Western Cengage Learning, 1/1/2012

DAVID SANDUA. 'HOW TO CREATE A SUCCESSFUL RURAL HOTEL.' Amazon Digital Services LLC - Kdp, 7/23/2023

Robert M. Schindler. 'Pricing Strategies.' A Marketing Approach, SAGE Publications, 9/15/2011

Oliver Raskin. 'The Handbook of Online Marketing Research: Knowing Your Customer Using the Net.' Joshua Grossnickle, McGraw Hill Professional, 10/2/2000

Stanislav Ivanov. 'Hotel Revenue Management: From Theory to Practice.' Zangador, 3/15/2014

Joshua D. Hayes. 'Revenue Management for the Hospitality Industry.' David K. Hayes, John Wiley & Sons, 11/9/2021

Robert G. Cross. 'Revenue Management.' Hard-Core Tactics for Market Domination, Crown, 4/27/2011